Sequoia and Kings Canyon National Parks

Museum Management Plan

2008

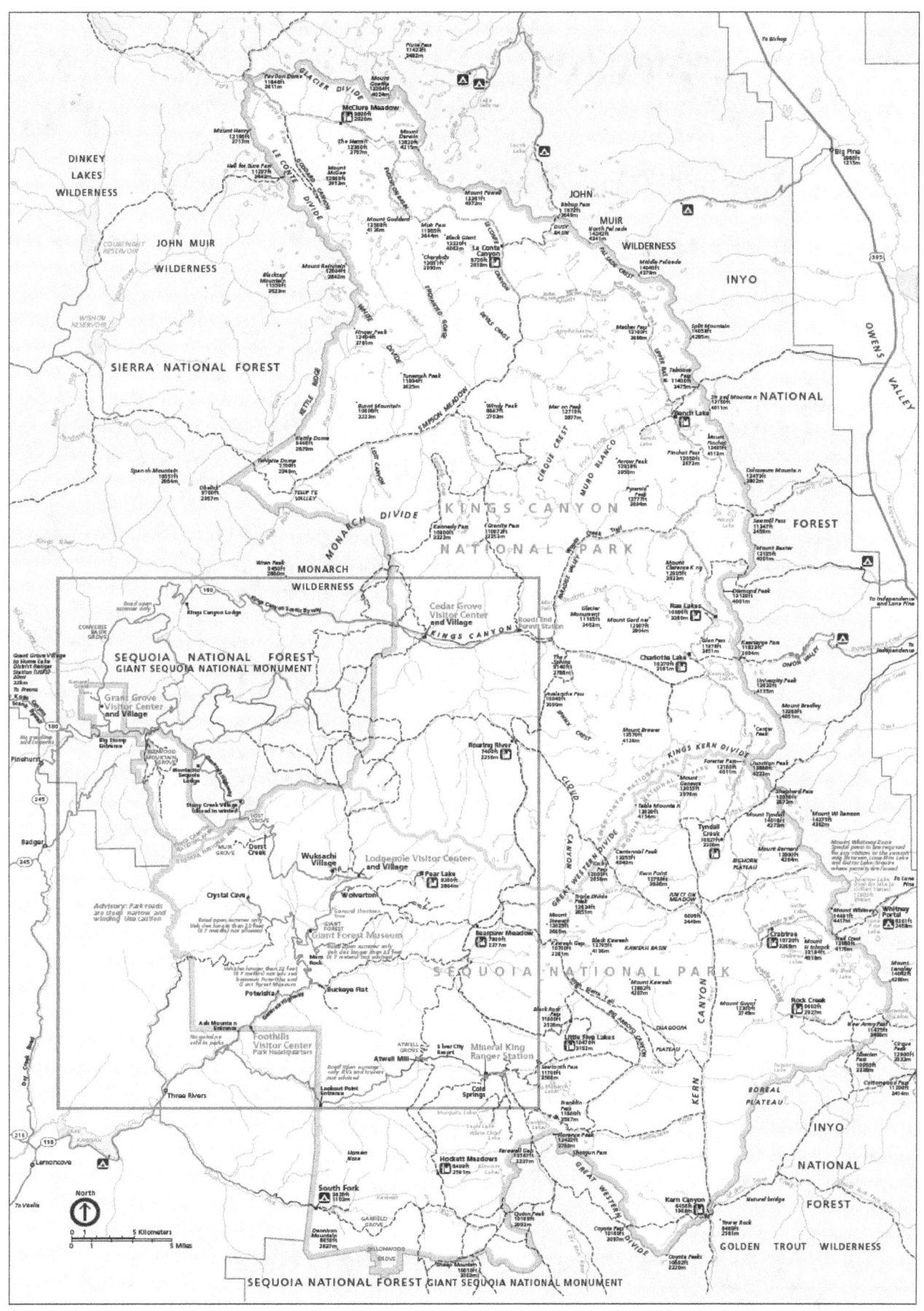

Sequoia and Kings Canyon National Parks

Museum Management Planning Team

Jonathan Bayless, Chief Curator
Yosemite National Park
Yosemite, California
(Team Leader)

Barbara Beroza, Museum Curator
Yosemite National Park
Yosemite, California

Richard Cronenberger, Historical Architect
Intermountain Regional Curatorial Collections Consultant
Denver, Colorado

Ward Eldredge, Curator
Sequoia and Kings Canyon National Parks
Three Rivers, California

Al Levitan, Conservator
Harpers Ferry Center
Harpers Ferry, West Virginia

Paul Rogers, Archivist
Yosemite National Park
Yosemite, California

Department of the Interior
National Park Service
Pacific West Region
2008

Sequoia and Kings Canyon National Parks

Museum Management Plan

2008

Recommended By:

[signature]   *January 14, 2008*

Diane L. Nicholson, Regional Curator   Date
Pacific West Region

Concurred By:

[signature]   1. Ap. 08

Craig Axtell, Superintendent   Date
Sequoia and Kings Canyon National Parks

Approved By:

[signature]   May 5, 2008

Jonathan B. Jarvis, Regional Director   Date
Pacific West Region

Executive Summary

The Sequoia and Kings Canyon museum collection is a marvelous resource that captures some of the excitement, diversity, history, and material culture reflecting the parks' rich heritage and biodiversity. This Museum Management Plan describes an approach for implementing improvements for the museum program over a five-year period that builds upon past achievements and anticipates future challenges.

This plan identifies the museum management challenges and opportunities that face the parks, and presents recommendations to advance the program. A survey of the park staff was conducted to determine current informational and program support needs. A team of museum management professionals developed this plan in cooperation with the staff responsible for managing park archives, museum collections, and library resources.

The archival and museum collections reflect the age and maturity of the parks. They are stored within the Visitor Center and other locations, with needs for additional investment and improvements. These important park-specific resources are efficiently contributing to park operations. The recent initiation of a regional and national strategy for museum facilities may challenge the parks to upgrade the museum program and justify its retention within the parks. The continued role and presence in the parks of museum and archive collections could be strengthened by reorganizing space and improving staffing and processing as defined herein. This Museum Management Plan is organized around the concept of meeting the challenge of the regional strategy and quickly achieving a level of facilities and staffing that will further demonstrate the commitment of the parks towards their museum collections.

The museum program can benefit from a variety of improvements within the next five years, including investments in the museum facilities used for storage, study and work space; progress on archive and records management;

an ongoing training process to achieve higher levels of professionalism; and programming for staffing by journeyman-level professional staff.

This Museum Management Plan offers recommendations for actions designed to upgrade and improve the organization and preservation of park archives and museum collections. Through incremental improvements, the parks will be in a position to meet the standards for a professionally-run museum facility and achieve designation as an accepted repository in the Pacific West Region and the National Park Service.

Key Recommendations

Key program recommendations are as follows. More detailed action recommendations follow each issue section of the plan.

- Use existing museum space to serve the program needs for the foreseeable future based upon the spatial and functional recommendations made in this plan and previous plans. This plan does not foresee pursuing a new museum facility in the short-term timeframe.

- Conduct an archival assessment and survey of existing records. Make corrections in the older system of archival organization, and process incoming records according to current standards.

- Revise and update necessary museum planning and programming documents, including the Scope of Collection Statement and budget requests to reflect the program needs.

- Identify and evaluate all museum materials and, where appropriate, complete accession and associated museum records to document museum property to current standards. Correct and update museum data on collection status and use.

- Implement the Preventive Maintenance Plan for storage and exhibit locations. Reorganize artifacts in collections storage facility.

Table of Contents

Cover Art

Front cover: Deadman Canyon, in what would become (in 1940) Kings Canyon National Park. Hand-colored photograph from the Roberts Collection, perhaps 1920s.

Front inside cover: Park map

Back inside cover: The first, temporary park museum. The image is dated to 1922, but may be 1924, and is credited to Lindley Eddy, the photo concessioner for Sequoia.

Back cover: Moro Rock with wooden steps built in the first year of NPS administration (1917). These were replaced with concrete steps in 1931. The photographer is not recorded.

List of Figures

List of Tables

The Museum Management Plan (MMP) replaces the Collection Management Plan (CMP) referred to in the National Park Service publications, *Outline for Planning Requirements, DO#28: Cultural Resources Management,* and the *NPS Museum Handbook,* Part I.

The CMP process generally concentrates on the technical aspects of museum operations, including a full review of accession files, status of cataloging, adherence to guidelines, and making very specific recommendations for corrections and improvements. In contrast, the MMP evaluates the museum programs within a park and makes a series of recommendations to guide development of park-specific programs that enhance the mission and goals of the park.

The MMP recognizes that specific directions for the technical aspects of archival and museum collections management exist within the *NPS Museum Handbook* series. The MMP does not, therefore, duplicate that type of information. Instead, the MMP places museum operations in context within park operations by focusing on how various collections may be used by park staff to support park goals. Recognizing that there are many different ways in which archives, libraries, and museum collections may be organized, linked, and used within individual parks, this plan seeks to provide park-specific advice on how this may be accomplished.

Prior to the site visit by the museum management planning team, park personnel were surveyed to collect baseline data concerning archival and museum collections, the library, and related services needed by the staff. This information allowed the team to make a quick evaluation of many issues related to these operations. The survey also provided insights into ways in which a well-designed museum management program might address the needs of the park staff. The results of this survey are contained in Appendix A.

The park staff and MMP team worked together over the course of the team's visit to develop the issue statements contained in this plan. Topics addressed meet the specific needs of Sequoia and Kings Canyon (SEKI) National Parks and do not necessarily cover every aspect of collection management concerns. The recommendations are intended to guide the parks through the process of implementing and enhancing a workable museum program that supports all aspects of park operations, while at the same time providing opportunities for growth and development of the museum and archive collection.

Members of the MMP team were selected for their ability to address the specific needs and concerns of the parks. Jonathan Bayless was the planning team leader and worked closely with the park to organize the team's site visit over a two-week period in September, 2005. While the team worked collaboratively to integrate the plan's approach, sections were written by individual authors. Authors were Ward Eldredge for the History of Collection Management, Rick Cronenberger for Issue A, Al Levittan for Issue B, Paul Rogers for Issue C and Appendices B and C, Barbara Beroza for Issue D, and Jonathan Bayless for Issue E and Appendix A.

The team wishes to thank the staff of Sequoia and Kings Canyon National Parks for the courtesy, consideration, and cooperation extended during this planning effort, in particular William C. Tweed, Chief of Interpretation, and Thomas L. Burge, Branch Chief of Cultural Resources Management. Their time, effort, and involvement have been very much appreciated, and made the team's job much easier. It is apparent that these individuals are dedicated and committed to the preservation of park resources.

1910s – 1920s

The organized collecting and exhibiting of natural history material at Sequoia National Park was already underway during the tenure of the first civilian superintendent, Walter Fry. In August of 1917, a wildfire destroyed Fry's Three Rivers residence and headquarters along with "over 4,000 specimens of the flora of the Sequoia and General Grant National Parks that had been collected and prepared for use in an exhibit of the flora of the parks." The collections were rebuilt and Fry's successor, Col. John R. White, reported at the end of the 1920 season that the floral displays that had been maintained in the entrance to the superintendent's office would "form the nucleus of the Park Museum, to be established when appropriation is available for the necessary building."

The responsibility for the collection of specimens and the preparation of exhibits was taken up by the nascent Nature Guide service, founded in 1919. By the middle of the 1922 season, the service had acquired and filled exhibition cases in the Administration Building at Giant Forest. Two summers later, as the search for a more permanent location continued, the collection had grown to the extent that the museum was temporarily housed in two tents in Giant Forest.

In May, 1925 the year-round administration of the park moved to Alder Creek, the original name for Ash Mountain, and the museum collections were returned to the vacated Administration Building at Giant Forest. The museum now shared the building with the checking office, a location considered advantageous as "the museum doubtless is visited by ninety-nine per cent of all tourists arriving at Giant Forest." This linkage of museum collections and general information services was deliberate. As Col. White explained to Director Horace Albright in January of 1925, "It is believed advisable to so bind the museum and Nature Guide work with the general information service that all park visitors will reach the museum building not as a side show but as the main center of attraction and information in the park."

Into this environment of provisional housing and persistent concerns for space, the museum received what is arguably its most valuable collection, comprising, then as now, the bulk of the museum's ethnographic holdings. In June of 1926, the park acquired an important collection of Native American material culture, which was donated by Jesse Agnew, a prominent citizen of Visalia and an early Sierra Club member, in memory of his late wife. The quality and value of this collection exacerbated concerns about fire and collections security. In the summer of 1929, as discussions over the construction of a permanent museum building continued, the baskets were stored in a shed in Giant Forest.

In correspondence with Ansel Hall, the Chief Naturalist for Yosemite National Park and a central figure in the Park Service's early museum program, White wrote that "We have reached the point in the development of our museum services to the public at which it is impossible to expand without a suitable building; as it is almost impossible to preserve those specimens which we have collected under present conditions." Through the late 1920s, White actively sought both public and private funding for the project. As late as 1931, Director Albright could concur, "In the case of Sequoia, it does seem as though there is real need for a fireproof museum to house the valuable Indian baskets and other objects collected by Judge Fry."

1930s

In 1933, the arrival of the Civilian Conservation Corps (CCC) inaugurated a period of extensive and controlled development in the Sequoia National Park. With CCC labor, ninety buildings were constructed and another sixteen rehabilitated, the park's total road mileage was doubled, and Crystal Cave was developed for visitation. Despite these developments, no new museum building was constructed. By the mid-1930s, Col. White had turned actively against the construction of a museum. In an exchange of letters with Assistant Director Bryant, White argued strongly against the relevance of museums to the National Park Service:

… I have seen throngs of people pouring through the museums in other national parks, ninety per cent of them at least seeking something to amuse them, looking at a stuffed bird indoors when they could go out of doors and hunt up the same bird if they knew how; many of them gazing just as they would along a Midway of a beach city; untrained to appreciate nature; eager for some new distraction, some way of putting in the time while in a national park. The kindest thing we can do for those people is to educate them in the out-of-doors by nature walks, at campfire lectures, and in the way we are doing out of doors. One of the most unkind things we can do is to try and duplicate in the national parks the sort of thing they visit in the cities.

Superintendent White's primary concern in the 1930s had become the moderation of development in Sequoia National Park, even its outright cessation in its fragile centerpiece, Giant Forest. For White, the presence of so many buildings amidst the sequoia groves seriously compromised the park's expressed mission. As he put it in an address to other park superintendents:

We are a restless people, mechanically minded, and proud of doing constructive work. Our factories, railroads, roads and buildings are admired by the world. We have in the parks a host of technicians, each anxious to leave his mark. But in all this energy and ambition there is danger unless all plans are subordinated to that atmosphere which though unseen, is no less surely felt by all who visit those eternal masterpieces of the Great Architect which we little men are temporarily protecting.

1940s

Under the next superintendent, Eivind Scoyen, the old Giant Forest Administration Building was renovated to serve permanently as the park's museum. In close contact with Dorr Yeager of the Park Service's newly centralized Western Museum Laboratories in Berkeley, a Museum Prospectus and Exhibit Plan for Sequoia was prepared by Park Naturalists Dr. Fritioff Fryxell and Frank Oberhansley. The report was approved, largely a *fait accompli,* in August of 1941 by the returning Superintendent White. The Prospectus defined for the museum's "central and dominant theme" the Giant Sequoias, and secondarily the geology and history of the park. The botanical specimens collected by Judge Fry and the other ranger naturalists—at the time constituting a third of the museum's holdings—were considered of relatively little importance:

Botanical features other than those relating to the Giant Sequoia can, despite their great interest, be interpreted adequately by other educational means, such as lectures, nature trails, and guided hikes.

It would appear that the bulk of Fry's herbarium was disposed of at this time; in the herbarium today there is only one specimen collected by Walter Fry, only fifty or so collected before 1940. While no records exist to document any exchange, park staff is currently attempting to determine if these collections might have been transferred to other herbaria in California.

While not all of its recommendations seem well-advised by today's standards, the Prospectus of 1941 marked the beginning of a formal museum management program for Sequoia National Park. Under Sequoia Park Naturalist Oberhansley, attempts were made to inventory and catalog museum holdings and to tighten the scope of the collections. For example, Arthur Woodward of the Los Angeles Museum was brought in to catalog the Agnew collection of Native American material culture; several items were identified as belonging to Plains cultures and were subsequently transferred to more suitable NPS units. Records created to document this transfer remain in the archives. This period also marks the acquisition of an important collection of negatives from early park photographic concessionaire, Lindley Eddy.

With the end of the Second World War, the production of the didactic exhibits recommended in the 1941 Prospectus, both at trailside and in the Giant Forest Museum, began in earnest. While Superintendent White remained against "a big building full of collections of butterflies, bugs, birds, beasts, etc.," by July of 1946, with only half of the proposed exhibits completed, the Giant Forest Museum had received some 15,625 visitors. The better part of the exhibit plan, including the obligatory large-scale relief model, were in place by the end of the summer of 1946.

1950s – 1970s

While the increased centralization of exhibit planning and construction within the Service assured the promotion of an orderly visitor experience, consistent collections management was longer in arriving. In 1955, the Park Service implemented the Museum Properties Management Act; the accession book currently in use at Sequoia and Kings Canyon dates to this period, evidently begun sometime between 1956 and 1958. Renewed interest in natural history collection outside the groves of sequoias also dates to this period. The herbarium began to grow, for the third time, through the efforts of park staff. A number of collections were made by Naturalist Samuel Pusateri. More systematic collections were made by two botanists, Jack Rockwell and Steve Stocking, who created the first vascular plant species list for the parks.

With Mission 66, new "visitor centers" were built at Grant Grove, Lodgepole, and Ash Mountain. In March of 1966, the Giant Forest Museum was closed: "After the exhibits were moved from the old Giant Forest Museum to the new Lodgepole Visitor Center, the Museum was stripped of any usable materials, then the building shell was bulldozed down and burned." By 1971, the museum contained 1,300 accessioned and cataloged objects under the administration of a park interpreter who had the duty of cataloging the backlog of objects and keeping the records up to date. In 1974, the collections were moved to the present location, in the basement of the Ash Mountain Visitor Center.

1980s to Present

In the mid-1980s, a concerted effort was made to bring the herbarium up to contemporary standards. Park Service Ecologist Larry Norris inventoried and cataloged the collection, identified specimens using Munz's nomenclature, and annotated voucher labels. This period also marks the beginning of large-scale, coordinated natural history collecting in the parks.

Norris, a trained photographer, also organized the parks' photo file, a collection of some 10,000 historic negatives dating from ca. 1890-1950: nitrate negatives were reformatted, prints were created, as well as a searchable database. The early accession of negatives from Sequoia Park photographic concessionaire Lindley Eddy was subsumed into this collection and includes some of its finest imagery.

In the late 1980s, the parks hired Ellen "Sissy" Seeley as museum curator. She had extensive experience and began a period of increased emphasis on the professional management of the parks' museum collections. Extensive work was conducted to bring the collections in line with Servicewide standards. Melanie Ruesch began working as a museum technician under Ellen Seeley and ran the program by herself after Seeley left. Ward Eldredge was hired in 1999 as a museum technician in his first position in the National Park Service. (Eldridge was upgraded to a GS-1015-09 Curator in 2006.)

Through the last decades of the twentieth century, natural and cultural history collections have continued to grow. Collections were generated through both park research projects and those of the Biological Resources Division of the United States Geological Survey. In May of 1992 and July of 1994, a National Park Service team visited the parks and produced the Collection Management Plan, approved in 1997.

More recent years have seen the cataloging of:

- The photo file
- The acquisition of a large and significant collection of photographs, negatives, and papers from Grant Park photographic concessionaire, Henry E. Roberts
- Substantial vascular plant collections associated with the current Rare Plants survey and Vegetation Mapping projects
- A collection of journals from one of the early civilian rangers from the first decades of the twentieth century

Figure 1   MMP Team member Barbara Beroza in the outer office of the museum.

Sequoia and Kings Canyon National Parks Museum Management Plan

Issue Statement

Improve the storage and protection of museum collections by increasing the organizational efficiency of the Ash Mountain Headquarters Facility, taking advantage of the good environmental conditions and fireproof building construction of the current storage space.

Background

Over the past several years, there have been many recommendations for improving the museum collection storage at Sequoia and Kings Canyon National Parks. Most of these recommendations have not been implemented, except for those that addressed the collection storage room. Not surprisingly, the NPS Checklist for Preservation and Protection of Museum Collections identifies a number of building and management deficiencies. The museum program has recently proposed constructing a new facility because the museum collection space appeared to be at capacity. It is the opinion of the MMP team that the current space can meet the needs of the museum program if it is reorganized and new space for staff offices is obtained.

The museum program occupies the following four rooms in the far northeast lower level of the Ash Mountain Headquarters Building:

- Collections storage room — 630 square feet (SF)

- The vault — 110 SF

- Darkroom — 130 SF

- Office/workroom — 300 SF

Altogether, these four rooms contain approximately 1,170 square feet. Two additional rooms of object storage space, which total 130 SF, are located in the warehouse. The overall organization workspace and collection storage operations have changed little since the 1997 CMP. Therefore, many of the

1997 observations and recommendations have not been repeated in this report, because for the most part, they are still valid.

Discussion

Current Museum Space Evaluation

In many ways the museum program is fortunate to be located in the lower level of the Ash Mountain Headquarters Building. The central collection storage room is situated partially underground and the substantial poured-in-place concrete walls, floors, and ceiling provide for excellent stable environmental conditions. The museum spaces are separated from the rest of the headquarters building with fire-resistant construction. The arrangement of the rooms facilitates good access and security controls and has the potential for offering a good, functional collections management program. The highly visible location in the center of park operations is also good for the program.

- **Central storage room.** The central storage room is the most efficient area of the museum program. The collection storage capacity is maximized in this trapezoidal space with the efficient use of Spacesaver™ mobile compact storage units and museum cabinetry. The storage units are arranged by object collection type and have been organized this way since 1997. (See the existing storage layout plan in Figure 2.)

- **Vault.** The vault, which is accessed through the collection storage room, has a fairly efficient layout.

- **Darkroom.** The darkroom is the most underutilized space in the program because it is used only a few times a year for non-museum related functions. The original darkroom operations should be removed.

- **Office/workroom.** The office/workroom contains multipurpose space and is the most dynamic space. This area serves as the main entry, office space for three staff, the workroom, workspace for researchers, office storage, file storage, textbook and reference manual storage, general storage, and the holding and receiving area for collections. In addition to the museum program functions, the cultural resource program also uses this space. Reorganizing and decompressing this space is a vital action to improving the curatorial program.

- **Warehouse storage rooms.** There are two small storage rooms in the park warehouse that function as holding spaces for collections. They have no active environmental controls and offer minimal protection to the collections stored there at this time.

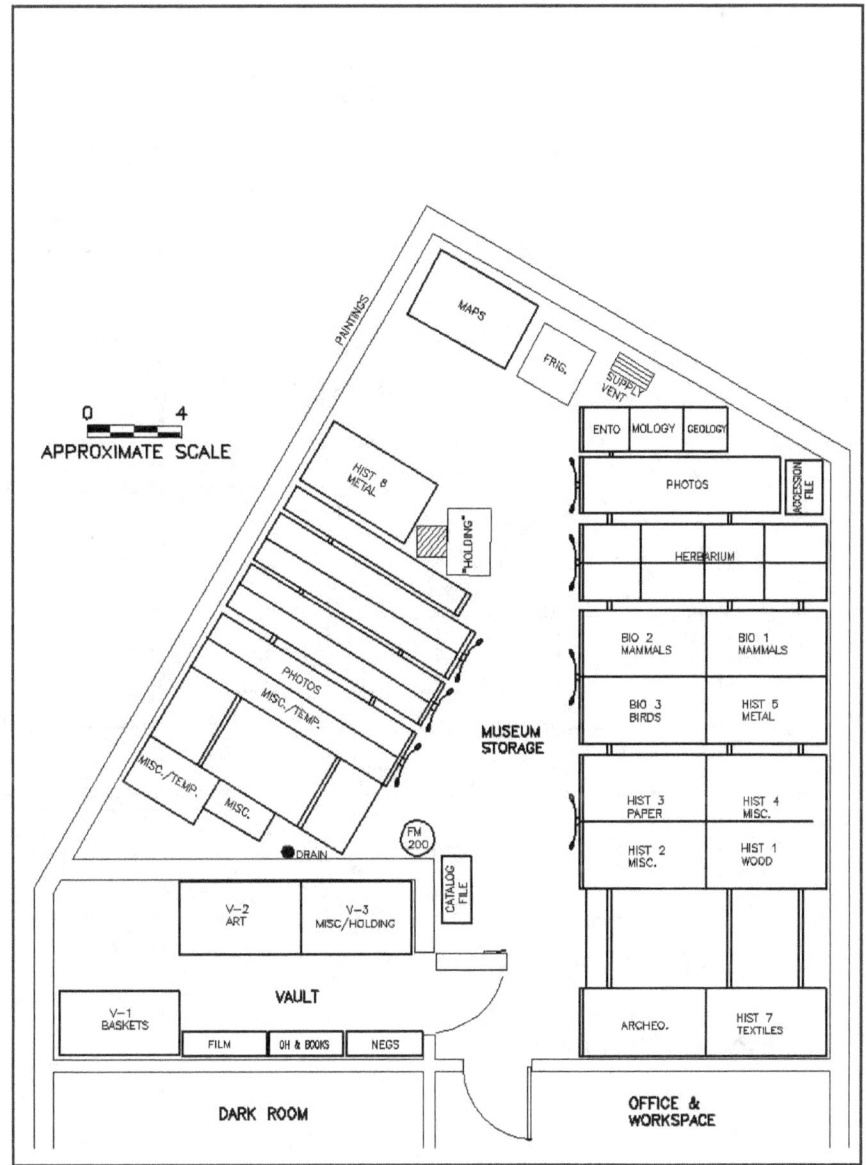

Figure 2   Existing layout of the SEKI museum space.

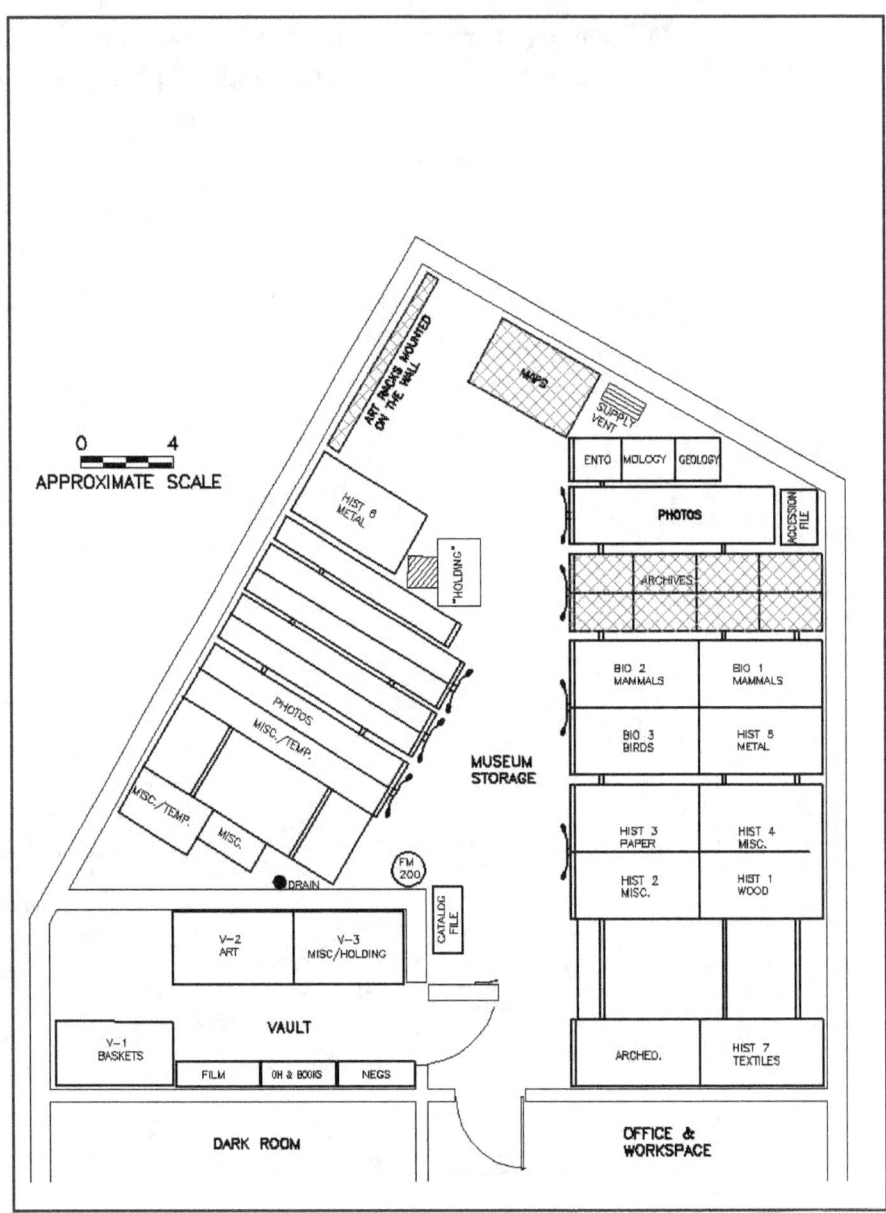

Figure 3   Proposed layout of the SEKI museum space.

Storage Volume Capacity

The collections are stored in modern museum cabinetry, both freestanding and installed on Spacesaver™ mobile storage units. The archive materials are stored in archive boxes on Spacesaver™ open shelves. The overall layout of the storage room is very efficient, considering that it is a trapezoidal shaped room (see Figure 2). Inspection of the individual storage cabinets reveals that space usage is approximately 50 to 60% of capacity. In other words, there is a 40 to 50% growth potential with the current collection equipment.

Rearranging the storage by type, association, monetary value, and potential use would increase the storage efficiency. (For more information, see the *Collection Management Plan* (1997), Chapter 5.)

Fire Detection and Suppression

The fire detection and suppression systems are monitored by the Park Dispatch office located in the same building. There is an FM-200 fire suppression system located in the collections storage rooms in addition to smoke detectors. The suppression system is under contract for inspection and is serviced twice a year. All the museum spaces have smoke detectors. It was noted that one of the collection room fire extinguishers was marked as last inspected in 1997. The headquarters building is scheduled to receive a wet-pipe fire-suppression system within the next two years.

Security System

The security system has not changed since the *Collection Management Plan* (1997). It consists of the electronic alarm system installed in 1994, electronic eye beams, and passive infrared motion detectors. The door to the storage room has a combination punch lock. All the museum cabinets are lockable, but they are rarely kept locked. The electronic eye beam that guards the entry door had piled material blocking the beam.

HVAC/Environment

The Ash Mountain climate is mild and wet in the winter and hot and dry in the summer, with winter temperatures averaging 40 to 50 degrees and summer temperatures averaging 75 to 100 degrees. The overall year-round relative humidity (RH) average level is approximately 35 to 40%. The lowest recorded exterior temperature was 17° and the highest was 117°. The temperature and relative humidity in the collections storage cannot be individually controlled by the museum program because their control is connected to the building-wide zoned system.

According to Bob Wood, the SEKI air-conditioning equipment mechanic, the 30-year-plus Heating, Ventilation, and Air Conditioning (HVAC) system is well-maintained and performs well even though it is original 1960s equipment. The makeup supply air is filtered to 40% efficiency and the filters are changed quarterly. All of the supply and return ducts were cleaned six years ago. It is a two-pipe system, which means that it is either only heating or cooling, providing heat during the winter and cooling during the summer. The pneumatic thermostat temperature control for the curatorial office space is located in the maintenance office. Mr. Wood manually manages the chiller during the shoulder seasons so that the office spaces stay as comfortable as possible. Since the building is occupied 24 hours a day, the HVAC system is operated all the time to keep the staff comfortable.

The temperature control for the collection spaces is located upstairs. The thermostatically-conditioned air is provided on demand to all the rooms through floor ducts. There is no humidity control in the system. There is one supply duct located in each museum space. The air is returned to the HVAC equipment through one ceiling duct located in each space. The return air from the first floor superintendent's offices, the library, and the visitor center spaces passes over the museum spaces in a fire-rated ceiling plenum. It is not known at this time what effect this return air stream may have on the museum environment.

However, given the limitations of the HVAC system, the overall internal environment in the collection storage space is fairly stable. The temperature stays about 70° all year with minor seasonal fluctuations. For the five-month period from April to September, temperature in the vault ranged from 68° to 74°F with a mean of 71°. Temperature in the storage room ranged from 66° to 74° with a mean of 69°. Relative humidity (RH) in the vault ranged from 31% to 49% with a mean of 43%, while in the store room the RH ranged from 18% to 45% with a mean of 34%. The excursion below 20% was short-lived. It appears that the RH rarely exceeds the identified museum management extremes, probably less that 1% of the year.

The exceptionally favorable local climatic conditions, as well as the solid and imperviously-constructed concrete rooms, contribute significantly to passively maintaining the internal environment. The potentially high exterior winter RH is mitigated by the need to heat the building, thus lowering the interior RH. The potentially low exterior summer RH levels are mitigated by the need to cool the building, thus raising the interior RH. However, the internal RH levels will continue to fluctuate in direct reaction to the outside conditions. For example, during the MMP team visit, a rain shower came through, and the RH temporarily increased from 38% to 45%. This short-term event is not preventable, nor is it detrimental to the collections (see Issue B for more discussion on conservation).

At one time, higher RH levels in the storage room was an issue, and NPS conservator Gretchen Voeks recommended closing off the return air duct (see the *Preventive Maintenance Plan* (2004), page 13). This resulted in a stabilization of the RH in the space, although the reason is not clearly understood. It also created a positive pressure in the space, with the primary pressure relief being through the entrance door, and the secondary relief through the small openings into the ceiling plenum. This change may have prevented unconditioned air from entering the collection storage room through the office workspace area and ceiling plenum.

The storage room environment is maintained in a relatively stable condition through combination of many factors; a change in any one of them could have a direct effect on the space. It is important that the temperature and RH are constantly monitored and any change in the conditions be recorded and the causes identified. The museum staff should also be aware of any changes proposed to the building-wide HVAC system. There have been recent funding requests to upgrade the system. Any change to the current system could have a drastic impact on the collections.

The NPS requires each park's museum management program to maintain and preserve their collections in the best possible condition. It is recognized that the ideal conditions cannot always be met. However, this does not necessarily mean that the collections are at a significant risk. By taking a practical and logical approach to evaluating the real risk to the collections, an informed decision can be made to correct or mitigate the highest risk conditions and still provide good long-term preservation.

Risk Assessment

One method to access risk to the collections is described in the *Framework for Preservation of Museum Collections* developed by the Canadian Conservation Institute. It helps to evaluate existing park storage conditions against the "Agents of Deterioration." The agents are listed here in rough order of importance for their potential of damaging artifacts. Identifiable threats specific to Sequoia & Kings Canyon museum collections are identified after each agent:

- **Direct Physical Forces:** This category addresses cumulative threats such as dropping and handling, or catastrophic events, such as earthquakes. The SEKI collections appear to have minimal risk in this category, because the accessioned collections are all in enclosed storage cabinets, with fairly good mounts and working doors. Consolidating the collections on each shelf would provide increased protection by preventing objects from sliding around. This risk can be mitigated with small incremental improvements in the SEKI collections storage rooms.

- **Thieves, Vandals, Displacers:** This category addresses the theft of small or portable objects or the unintended misplacement of objects by staff. This threat is a real risk to the SEKI collections due to the extensive backlogged accessioning concerns (see Issue C) and the unorganized and crowded office area with multiple piles of backlogged collections, office work, and other activities occurring in this single space (see *Collection Storage Plan draft,* 1997). This threat can be prevented by creating a dedicated workroom with more controlled access and separate from the day-to-day office functions, and by eliminating record-keeping backlogs.

- **Fire:** The loss of collections by fire is a high risk; however, the risk of a fire occurring at the SEKI collections room itself is very low. The primary SEKI threat is most likely from a structural fire originating outside the space in other rooms or the mechanical room causing smoke or heat damage. The risk of a structural fire will be greatly reduced when the headquarters building-wide fire suppression system is installed in the near future. Quick response by law enforcement and fire crews is equally important.

- **Water:** The level of threat to SEKI museum collections from obvious day-to-day water damage is very low. However, the possibility of catastrophic damage is very high if a fire occurs in the visitor, library, or superintendent's office areas. Great quantities of water would flow from the fire hoses through the floor-mounted return air ducts directly into the collections storage room. This threat can be mitigated by clearly identifying this risk in the *Structural Fire Plan* and developing a *Museum Collections Disaster Management Plan.*

- **Pests:** Pest threats include insects, beetles, and rodents. There is an ongoing pest infestation problem in the collections storage room (for more information, see the *Collection Management Plan* (1997), page 29, and the *Preventive Maintenance Plan* (2004), page 14). The primary entry point appears to be through the return air ducts located in the ceiling plenum. This problem can be prevented by screening the building-wide return air ducts in the ceiling plenum, and it can be mitigated by careful monitoring for occurrence by trapping.

- **Contaminates:** Possible contaminates consist of airborne pollens, dust, and pollution. External sources of contaminates do not appear to be getting into the museum collection room. The supply air is filtered to at least 40% and the collection room has a positive pressure most of the time, which limits any dust and pollen infiltration through the doors. Very little dust was observed on the surfaces of the cabinets. The ceiling tiles appear to be deteriorating slightly, which is causing some dust buildup. This could be prevented by sealing the tiles' surface with latex paint.

- **Radiation:** Ultraviolet and visible light can cause irreversible damage to museum collections. This type of damage can be prevented by keeping collections enclosed in cabinets, closed shelving, and containers, and not locating collections directly in sunlight. The threat from radiation damage at SEKI is extremely low at this time.

- **Incorrect Temperatures and Incorrect Relative Humidity:** Temperature and RH are interrelated and always need to be considered together. The SEKI climate is very favorable for collection preservation. The year-round RH averages are 36% to 40%, with seasonal lows into the teens and highs into the high 50% range. The climate is mild and wet in the winter with average temperatures of about 60°, and is hot and dry in the summer with several days over 100°. The HVAC system does a very good job providing a stable nonfluctuating year-round temperature of 70° to 74° (see HVAC discussion in this issue). The potential damage to collections from the natural and controlled levels of temperature and RH at SEKI is low. However, the artificial threat is somewhat higher because the internal temperatures are dependent upon the building HVAC system which is outside the control of the museum program.

NPS Museum Collection Facility Model

The NPS Facility Planning Model was run to determine the predicted size of a new facility that would serve the parks' museum program needs for the next 25 years. The model identifies the appropriate functional and square footage needs based on the size of the collection, the storage requirements, and staffing.

The model predicted a new facility sized at approximately 2,900 square feet. This is approximately 2.4 times larger than the current space. It consists of:

1. Staff areas—720 net SF

2. Public areas—370 net SF

3. Processing areas—170 net SF

4. Object and archive storage—988 net SF

5. Additional photographic storage space—100 net SF

The area remaining (TARE) at 20% totals 562 net SF. The estimate to construct a facility of this size would be approximately $2,000,000 based on 2005 costs and a 6% inflation rate. The estimate could change significantly depending upon the actual site development cost.

CCC Proposal

The museum program has been considering moving the museum collection to the historic Civilian Conservation Corps (CCC) barracks at the Sycamore site. This move would require both rehabilitation and new construction. The Program Management Information System (PMIS) Project Statement 5710 requested $100,000 to plan and design the facility. In addition, PMIS Project Statement 75971 requests $600,000 for construction of the proposed facility. Although the idea of reusing an abandoned historic structure for a new use is commendable, it is the opinion of the MMP team that this is not a solution the museum program should pursue for a number of reasons:

- The 75-foot long by 20-foot wide CCC structure has approximately 1,500 SF and would require a substantial new addition or additional building to meet the predicted program size of 2,900 SF.

- The wooden frame structure would be more at risk from fire and pests.

- The structure is somewhat isolated from the major park operations, such as fire and security.

- The move would decrease the visibility of the museum program and potentially reduce collection use.

- The external environment contains significantly more dust and biological pests than the headquarters area.

- Perhaps most importantly, there would be little if any cost difference between rehabilitating the CCC structure and building a completely new facility.

The current location at the Ash Mountain Headquarters building, if recommendations proposed in this and past plans are implemented, could serve the museum program needs for the foreseeable future. The improvements should be easily accomplished using the budget of the proposed and approved $100,000 planning project.

Improving Existing Space

Even though the Facility Model predicted a facility 2.4 times larger than the existing space, it does not necessarily mean that the current space is inadequate. As described above, the building structure system, fire-resistant construction, layout, and environmental conditions are very good. The fire protection and security systems work well. The greatest weakness is the layout and functional use of the existing spaces. The darkroom is an under-used space and the workroom/research room/office function is extremely inefficient. The primary museum functions that are missing or under-allocated from current museum spaces are a dedicated work area, research room, and accession and processing space. (CMP 1997, CSP draft 1997.)

Evaluation of Existing Space

How does the existing space compare to the Facility Planning Model prediction? This comparison can be seen in Table 1 on the next page, with explanatory notes following the table.

Curatorial Program Functions	Model Net SF	Park Net SF	Difference	Comments	Park % utiliza-tion	Shortfall Net SF
a. Core Functions: workstations, offices, file storage	480	150	330	Non-museum office space in one area.	30%	330
b. Restrooms, break room, recycle space	240	0	0	Provided by existing building.		
c. Processing areas, workroom, material storage, receiving and holding	170	150	20	Too many functions in one space.	70%	20
d. Public areas and research space	370	0	370	Essential, not often used.		0
e. Objects and archives storage	988	740	248	The storage cabinets are underutilized.	50%	0
f. Archive storage				Archives spaces are combined with objects.		0
g. Photographic storage	100	0	100	This is a desired space.		0
h. Darkroom	0	130	130	This space should be used for processing and holding.	35%	0
i. Other						
Total Net SF	**2348**	**1170**	**1198**			**350 NSF.**
TARE/HVAC	587					
Estimated Gross SF	2935					
Recommendation						

Table 1 Evaluation of the SEKI museum collections program space compared with the facility planning model results and actual use analysis (10/12/05).

The Ash Mountain Headquarters building location could serve the museum program needs for the foreseeable future, if recommendations proposed in this and past plans are implemented. They should be able to be accomplished within the proposed and approved $100,000 planning project, or alternatively, from other funding sources.

a. Core Functions: The existing workroom area has the greatest functional conflicts due to its small size and all of the functions and activities it must support. As Table 1 shows, it is over 100% undersized. However, if the office and non-museum program functions were relocated to other spaces in the headquarters area, this approximately 240 total SF will reduce the deficiency to 140 SF, which is a much more workable situation. Additional space efficiency could be obtained by installing efficient systems office furniture.

b. Restrooms and Break Room: These functions are currently provided in the Headquarters building.

c. Processing Areas: These functions would be more efficiently accommodated in a redesigned workroom. Some of the functions would be located in the reused darkroom space.

d. Public Areas and Research Space: The research space would be accommodated in the redesigned workroom.

e. Objects and Archives Storage: The current storage capacity is up to 50% underused. This potential storage capacity significantly offsets the storage space difference of 488 SF.

f. Archives Storage: The archives storage space is co-located in the object storage space in this facility. (See item e. Objects and Archives Storage.)

g. Photographic Storage: This space was added to the curatorial facility model because it is a specialized use. However, moving the nitrate negatives to San Francisco Maritime National Historical Park (SAFR) or Western Archeological and Conservation Center (WACC) would provide more efficient storage for this resource. The photographs could use a better microclimate, but at this time it is not crucial to their long-term preservation. The photographic survey recommended by this plan may offer additional recommendations.

h. Darkroom: This space can be reassigned to other functions. The darkroom function can be retired, with either digital photo copies or photo duplication contracted to outside businesses. It is shown for comparison against the functions not provided in the current facility.

i. TARE/HVAC: These functions and space allocation are currently provided within the current Headquarters building.

Spatial Alternatives

Any number of possible layouts could improve the curatorial office / workroom and darkroom space. Two alternatives are presented in Figure 4 to illustrate the conceptual reorganization of these two rooms as discussed herein. The herbarium cabinets would be moved into the workroom, with dedicated research and processing areas. This change would improve accessibility to these collections and resolve some collection security concerns. The darkroom would function as collections holding, dirty storage, and some processing. The rolling layout table provides more flexibility in altering the workroom for specialized tasks. The success of these proposals is dependent upon selecting furniture and cabinets that are specifically designed and sized for the required functions and efficiently maximizing the use of the existing space.

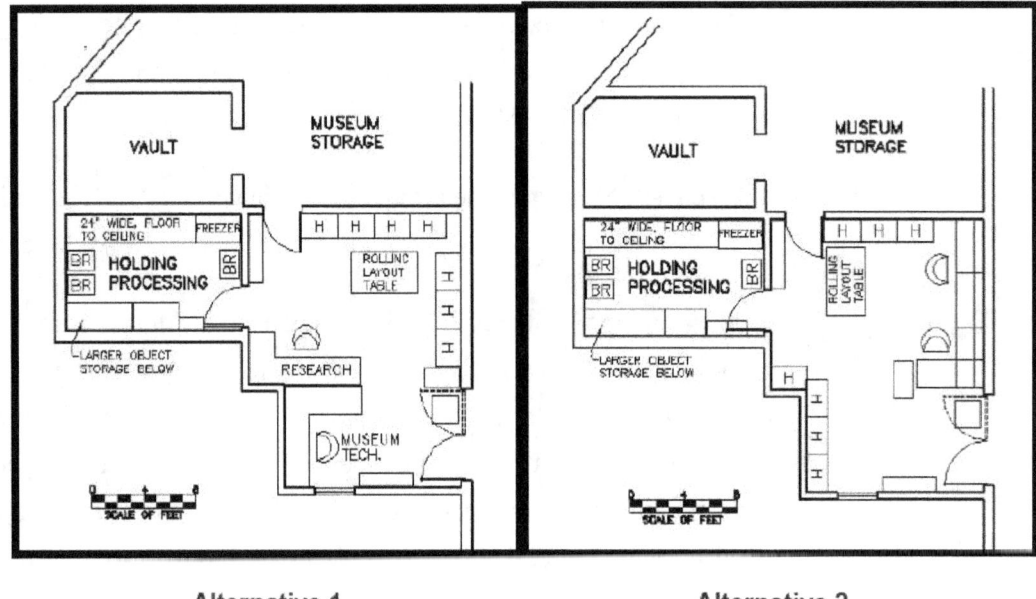

Alternative 1   Alternative 2

Figure 4 Redesign of layout of current museum office and darkroom.

Alternative 1 is the preferred recommendation. The museum technician's desk at the entryway offers a greater sense of security and oversight in the space. The artifacts are located further away from the door, and the desk layouts are separated, which helps to distinguish between visitor and management.

The following narrative describes the specific changes that should occur in each space to make it more efficient.

- **Darkroom:** All the darkroom equipment, work counter, and cabinets would be removed.

- **North wall**: New floor-to-ceiling, 24-inches deep, 7 rows high, 11-feet long steel shelving installed along the north wall. The total shelving area would be 154 SF. The freezer would remain in its current location, and the top of it would double as a temporary layout space. Three rows of 12-inch deep wall-mounted shelves would be above the freezer for collection material supply storage. These shelves could be cabinets with doors instead.

- **South wall:** New 9-foot long, 24-inch deep shelving unit for large object storage. Large, open areas in the shelf unit would accommodate large objects such as the wheelbarrow and signs. An area on top of shelves would be designated for box storage. One small 12-inch deep, 3-foot wide, 7- or 8-shelf unit for storage would be installed. Total of 24 SF of shelving. Storage for a 1- to 3-foot by 5-foot folding table behind the door. Three baker's racks, on wheels, for archive or backlog in progress work. These racks can be rolled around and in and out of the workroom as they are being worked on.

- **Workroom/research room**: This space would be devoted only to the museum collection function, serving jointly as the workroom/processing room and research room. The museum technician and research work areas would consist of systems furniture, with 24-inch deep work surfaces, wall or panel-mounted shelving above the work surface, file cabinets, and drawers under the work surfaces. The herbarium cabinets would be located in this space: 10 short cabinets stacked and 2 tall cabinets. This is a tight fit, but would help provide park biologists direct access to this collection independent of the cultural collection. A new rolling table for research and collections processing could be used. Floor-to-ceiling shelves (5-feet long and 7-shelves high) for reference books on the wall next to the collections storage room door would provide 35 linear feet of shelving. A floor-to-ceiling bookcase or combination lateral files and bookcase would be located on the south wall near the door. The nitrate negative refrigerator would be relocated to this room, positioned directly in front of the unused leaf of the double entrance door. The fireproof safes would be located in this room.

- **Collections storage room:** The relocation of the herbarium cabinets will allow for expansion of the archive storage and some improved reorganization of the room. The map case would be relocated to the refrigerator location and an art rack would be installed on the west wall to more efficiently hang the art. The mobile compact storage units that held the herbarium could be modified or replaced to hold archive material. Making other substantial modifications to the mobile compact storage units is a higher-cost approach, and should be considered a lower priority than the other changes at this time.

Recommendations

- The MMP team recommends using the Fee Demo funding recently approved by the parks for planning and design ($100,000) and reallocating it to correcting the identified deficiencies. Alternatively, funds from Cultural Cyclic Maintenance or Museum Collections Protection and Preservation Program (MCPPP) funding might be used.

- Move the three staff office functions to another location in the parks, or possibly retain only the curator in the current space.

- If feasible, utilize part of the existing Audiovisual (AV) room, located adjacent to the break room. If it can be reorganized and used, whole or in part, the AV room could house supplies, collection receiving, and holding storage, and/or it could perhaps be a workspace or office.

- Eliminate the darkroom function and remove the equipment from the room. This is essential space for reuse.

- Purchase systems furniture for the workspace.

- Retrofit the storage space in the warehouse to provide a more stable environment for holding non-archive collections for accessioning.

- Reorganize the workroom space. Relocate the herbarium to the workroom.

- Purchase additional Spacesaver™ units for archival storage.

- Move the nitrate collections to SAFR or WACC and eliminate the need for cold storage.

- Paint all of the ceilings with a white titanium latex paint to consolidate the friable ceiling tile surface and provide additional ultraviolet (UV) protection.

- For pest control, install ¼-inch (metal) carpenter cloth across the HVAC visitor center wing return air duct to prevent mice and large insects from entering the museum storage area. Install it so that it can be easily opened to remove trapped and dead insects and rodents. Install ¼-inch (metal) carpenter cloth across the HVAC return air duct where it enters the mechanical room from the plenum above the workroom area. Install ¼-

inch (metal) carpenter cloth on the inside of the return air duct grills in the visitor center, library, and superintendent's office spaces. Note that window screen would restrict airflow, so it should not be used.

- Actively record and evaluate the temperature and relative humidity with data loggers. Install data loggers in the rooms and in cabinets, and install one on the exterior of the space to record the outside climatic conditions. The exterior information would serve as the climatic baseline allowing for accurate evaluation of how much protection the structure, rooms, cabinets, and HVAC systems are providing to the collections and for developing solutions (also see Issue B).

Figure 5 The Alles cabin at Mineral King.

Sequoia and Kings Canyon National Parks Museum Management Plan

Issue B — Collection Preservation

Issue Statement

Implementing sound preventive and remedial conservation strategies for the museum collections of Sequoia and Kings Canyon National Parks will help ensure long-term preservation of these resources for research and use. Improvement can be made through realization of both short- and long-term strategies and goals.

Background

The museum collections in Sequoia and Kings Canyon reflect the natural and social history of the southern Sierra Nevada Mountains. A central mission of the parks' museum program is to preserve collections, whether in storage, exhibit, or on loan. Some significant steps have been taken in the implementation of both preventive and remedial conservation since the *Collection Management Plan* was approved in 1997; however, additional improvement in both operations and facilities is needed to ensure long-term preservation of the collection.

In the development of this plan, a number of previous studies and plans were reviewed to understand the parks' collections management history. They addressed both broad preservation concerns and conservation of individual artifacts. The documents relevant to this chapter include:

- *SEKI Collection Management Plan*, Bayless et.al., 1997
- *SEKI Scope of Collection Statement*, 2004
- *SEKI Collections Storage Plan*, Bush et al., 1997
- *SEKI Collection Condition Survey*, Voeks and Katterman, 1997
- *SEKI Preventive Maintenance Plan*, Eldredge, 2004

Preventive and Remedial Conservation

Preservation of collections entails both remedial and preventive conservation. Remedial conservation treatment attempts to stabilize an object by rectifying structural and chemical damage and slowing any future deterioration. In some cases, restoration—the return of an object to an earlier appearance—is appropriate to allow the viewer to better appreciate the aesthetic intent of the maker or to place it in historical context. Remedial treatment is often labor-intensive and costly.

Preventive conservation is in essence providing an environment that is conducive to the long-term survival of an artifact or an entire collection. Creation of such an environment can reduce or eliminate the need for remedial conservation. To some extent, preventive conservation has been practiced for as long as humans have had possessions they value; it often involves simply good housekeeping, maintenance, and the exercise of common sense. Modern science-based conservation has refined and quantified preventive conservation by identifying the causes of object deterioration and providing standards and solutions to environmental problems.

From a broader perspective, preventive conservation can also include protection against fire, flood, theft, and vandalism. All of these factors potentially impact collections more rapidly and significantly than can environmental agents of deterioration. Therefore, from a risk management standpoint, these agents should receive serious attention and long-term funding.

Although many preventive conservation measures such as environmental monitoring, curatorial housekeeping, and Integrated Pest Management (IPM) are relatively simple and straightforward, to be effective they must be carried out on a regular and continuing basis. The need for an ongoing commitment of staff time should not be underestimated.

At this juncture in the development of the museum program, preventive conservation should be one of the priorities of the SEKI cultural resource staff. These efforts will benefit the entire collection by minimizing the environmental causes of deterioration and thereby reducing the need for future treatment intervention. In cases where remedial conservation treatment is warranted, the work should be performed by experienced and trained conservators working in their particular area of expertise.

Environmental Concerns

Environmental concerns fall into four categories: temperature and relative humidity, light, dust and air pollution, and pests. Each of these concerns is discussed below.

Temperature and Relative Humidity

High temperatures and relative humidity accelerate chemical aging of materials. Fluctuations in relative humidity (RH), and to a lesser extent temperature, can result in mechanical damage to organic materials. Where long-term fluctuations over the course of weeks or months may be tolerated without damage, shorter-term fluctuations can result in mechanical failure. Extremes in RH also cause damage, particularly on the high end, which promotes mold growth and increases the likelihood of insect infestation. Low RH can cause embrittlement and shrinkage of organic materials and failure of restrained elements and adhesives.

Objects, to an extent, become acclimated to their past environment. In the case of the SEKI collection, that environment has been one of moderately low levels of RH. Placement in an environment with the generic "ideal" RH of 50% (+/- 2%) could prove counterproductive. Lower RH levels are in fact beneficial for metals and most paper-based materials, which comprise a significant portion of the SEKI collection.

Light

Light, both visible and UV, is another environmental agent of deterioration of collections. The *NPS Museum Handbook* provides light level standards for different types of materials. In general, organic materials such as basketry and textiles are more sensitive to light than inorganic materials.

Light damage is cumulative, and the extent of damage is dependent on both intensity and duration. Because the duration of light in storage is usually short and artifacts are typically housed within cabinets or shelving, light intensity in storage facilities is generally not a critical factor. In fact, it is advantageous to have high light levels in storage areas, on demand, to be able to assess the condition of artifacts and any potential environmental problems.

The light sources in both exhibit and storage areas should not include any UV light—that portion of the light spectrum that is most damaging to materials but which the human eye cannot discern. Fluorescent lights typically have a high percentage of UV light; however, this can be controlled with the use of UV filtering sleeves or special purpose tubes. Glazing that eliminates the UV portion of the light spectrum can be used in windows and exhibit cases.

Dust and Air Pollution

Materials are subject to deterioration from particulates as well as air borne gaseous pollution. Dust is a particular problem in the furnished historic structures such as the Alles cabin, due to the nature of the building and the difficulty in keeping outside dust sources from entering. Dust acts as an abrasive, serves as a food source for insects, and helps create a microclimate of elevated RH in proximity to objects. Reducing the level of dust on artifacts on open exhibit and in unsealed exhibit cases requires regular curatorial housekeeping.

Pollution from the burning of carbon fuels by automobiles, coal-fired power plants, or wood smoke is an issue that affects many types of park resources. Photochemical smog, resulting from the effect of sunlight on car exhaust, is a potentially serious preservation concern, as it produces ozone, a strong oxidizing agent. Car exhaust also produces sulfur dioxide, sulfuric acid, and nitrogen dioxide, all highly acidic in nature and potentially deleterious to cultural artifacts. Chemical scavengers and filtering agents such as activated charcoal can be used in sealed exhibit and storage enclosures to reduce the effects of pollutants on sensitive materials.

Pests

Museum pests such as rodents, wood-boring beetles, and Dermestid beetles can damage artifacts in a short period of time, making regular and frequent monitoring for their presence necessary. This monitoring is particularly important for organic materials such as the basketry, paper, photographs, and textiles found in the SEKI collections.

Environmental Monitoring Program

The collection of environmental data (temperature, RH, light) is an important element in preventive conservation planning. Where there is an existing environmental control system, the data is used to gauge its performance and to determine if it is operating within the target range. For storage and exhibit areas with little or no control, the data can be used to relate environmental conditions to artifact condition and can help determine the type and extent of climate control needed. Although data from daily and monthly periods can be useful to assess short-term changes or malfunctions in HVAC equipment, for planning purposes the data should extend over a one-year cycle.

Data loggers are now available that provide a real-time digital readout as well as extensive memory capability. Real-time readout allows park staff to assess current conditions without having to download data. This can be of particular importance for loggers that are placed in exhibit cases. Some newer loggers utilize flash cards to transmit data from the logger to a computer, eliminating the need to bring the logger to a desktop computer or carry a laptop to the logger, an important consideration for park units with widely-dispersed exhibit and storage locations.

SEKI currently has two operational data loggers along with quite a few dial hygrometers and recording hygrothermographs. The data loggers are about ten years old and nearing the end of their useful lifespan.

Many dial hygrometers were found placed horizontally in storage areas on shelving units and within storage cabinetry, a position in which they are unable to measure RH accurately. They should be hung vertically for accurate measurement. Dial hygrometers drift out of calibration frequently and should be recalibrated with a good-quality electronic hygrometer on a regular basis, or simply replaced with digital data loggers.

The parks' recording hygrothermographs should be retired from use. Although they can, if calibrated frequently, create an accurate visual depiction of environmental conditions, they require extensive staff attention and do not provide interpretation of the data. Data loggers are more effective in recording and interpreting environmental data and require less staff time, and the associated software can interpret the data in a variety of useful ways.

Light meters are used to record visible light and UV light intensity. Currently very few organic materials are on display in the SEKI exhibit spaces, so measurement of light intensity is not a critical monitoring activity. In the event that sensitive organic materials are placed on exhibit, SEKI should utilize a light meter to ensure that light levels do not exceed NPS standards.

Conservation History

Remedial conservation treatment of SEKI artifacts has been done by the conservation staff of both Harpers Ferry Center (HFC) and the Western Archeological and Conservation Center (WACC). In 1975, the HFC metals conservator treated 23 objects (primarily metal) onsite as they were slated for exhibit in the Lodgepole Visitor Center. At that time, other objects were identified as needing laboratory treatment and four were treated in the HFC labs in 1976. Park staff was instructed in the care of artifacts, and other materials were sent to HFC for their treatment. During this time period, an HFC museum specialist visited to help organize collections in the vault.

Archeological, historical, and natural history specimens were treated and prepared at Harpers Ferry Center for the Kings Canyon exhibit in 1985. During the planning for the exhibits at the Giant Forest Museum, HFC conservators advised contract exhibit designers and park staff on preservation of wood cross-sections.

Conservators from the NPS Western Archeological and Conservation Center in Tucson, Arizona performed a Collection Condition Assessment in 1997. Their report included an assessment of environmental conditions of both storage and exhibit areas, as well as a condition survey of 193 objects in the collection. Four projects that included remedial and preventive conservation were developed. Remedial treatment was recommended for some items in the basketry collection, the textiles in the Buchanan collection, objects on exhibit at the Lodgepole Visitor Center, and selected high-priority items in the Ash Mountain museum storage. Many of these projects appear to have been carried out to some extent. Documentation of the treatment has not been found in the parks' files.

Discussion

Collection storage areas at the Ash Mountain Headquarters building and warehouse, exhibits in the Foothills, Lodgepole, and Grant Grove Visitor

Centers, and collections on temporary exhibit in the superintendent's office suite and furniture in the Alles Cabin were assessed for this plan. Potential collection materials at the Mineral King Ranger Station and the Ash Mountain Management office complex were also assessed. Many of the preservation-related deficiencies observed have been previously noted in 1997 in the *Collection Management Plan*, the *Collections Storage Plan* draft, and the *Collection Condition Survey*. Although some steps have been taken to comply with the recommendations of these previous reports, much work still needs to be done to assure the long-term preservation of the SEKI collection.

SEKI has a number of different exhibit locations; however, the number of artifacts on exhibit and their preservation needs are relatively small compared with the preservation needs of the collection in storage. With few exceptions, the objects on exhibit are robust in nature and not particularly sensitive to environmental conditions. Many objects are made of iron and solid, unfinished wood that can withstand fairly high light levels and a comparatively wide range of temperature and RH conditions (note, of course, that they are not impervious to threats such as direct water contact or theft).

With the exception of the Alles cabin, the permanent exhibits are within visitor centers. All the artifacts on exhibit, except those at the Grant Grove Visitor Center, are protected by display cases. Although these cases are far from ideal, they do provide a basic measure of security and protection from environmental agents of deterioration. Most of the artifacts currently on open exhibit at the Grant Grove Visitor Center are slated to be placed in storage when new exhibits are installed. (Note: The exhibits were changed in 2006.)

Collections storage is located in the Ash Mountain Headquarter Building and in two small rooms in the warehouse. The Ash Mountain collections space is divided between the vault and the main collection storage area, which is adjacent to the cultural resources office space (see Issue A). Specific preservation concerns for each of the exhibit and storage facilities are discussed below.

Exhibits

Foothills Visitor Center

The Foothills Visitor Center (Ash Mountain) exhibit contains a single display case that houses a Native American basket and granite cobble within an acrylic vitrine. The vitrine is alarmed and wired to the park dispatch office. The basket has a flat bottom surface that rests on a thin acrylic sheet shaped to conform to the configuration of the bottom. The acrylic acts as a barrier between the basket and the plywood case deck. The case has no silica gel buffering capability. It is illuminated with ambient light and overhead track lighting. At midday, light intensity measured at the outer surface of the vitrine was approximately 10-12 foot candles. Actual light intensity hitting the basket is reduced somewhat by the acrylic vitrine. Temperature was 78° F and the RH was 28% during a spot reading.

The basket appears to be in stable condition; however, vibration has caused it to move off of the acrylic barrier disk toward the back of the vitrine. A different barrier material with a less slippery surface should be substituted. Alternatively, the acrylic disk can be covered with fabric or thin, closed-cell ethafoam (Volara). The *Collection Condition Survey* noted that light levels on the basket were too high. It appears that the overhead track lighting has been adjusted to reduce light directed on the case and light intensity is currently acceptable.

The interior surface of the basket is somewhat dusty. It should be carefully cleaned under low suction with a high efficiency particulate air filter (HEPA) vacuum. This probably will be necessary on a yearly basis. The parks should purchase micro tools for the vacuum to perform curatorial cleaning tasks such as this.

The interpretative label does not refer specifically to the basket in the display case. The parks should consider removing this particular object and replacing it with a similar basket if one is available in the collection. "Resting" sensitive objects such as this minimizes the slow deterioration caused by exposure to light and dust that is inevitable while on exhibit.

Basketry is particularly sensitive to the environmental conditions, as the fibers respond to changes in relative humidity by absorbing and giving off moisture, which results in swelling and shrinking. Because of this sensitivity, the parks should consider either retrofitting the existing case to incorporate silica gel buffering or replacing the case with one that has a silica gel buffering compartment and UV filtering acrylic vitrine.

Lodgepole Visitor Center

Exhibits in the Lodgepole Visitor Center, which interpret the human history of the park, were installed in the mid-1970s. With the exception of a quilt that is hung on the wall of the outer room, all artifacts are housed in display cases. The original exhibit included both original and reproduction photographs. As recommended in the previous CMP, all of the photographs were reproduced and the originals placed in storage.

Thirty-eight objects are displayed, essentially without interpretation, in a large floor-mounted case. The case has no internal lighting or silica gel compartment. The objects are simply placed flat on the case deck. They were initially treated on-site in 1975 by an HFC conservator. Treatment consisted primarily of cleaning and coating ferrous surfaces with micro-crystalline wax. The *Collection Condition Assessment* of 1997 noted some corrosion on the ferrous surfaces beneath the wax coating and the presence of active corrosion on one of the lead bullets. It recommended re-treatment consisting of cleaning and removal of the old wax coatings, mechanical removal of corrosion, and re-application of micro-crystalline wax. This treatment was subsequently done for high-priority objects. Objects of lesser priority should also be programmed for treatment.

Environmental conditions are not currently recorded in the exhibit area. A data logger with digital read-out should be placed in the case.

The visible surfaces of most of the ferrous objects appear to be stable. One of the guns does exhibit some corrosion. All should be examined closely by a conservator experienced in weapons conservation to determine the need for treatment. This determination often requires that the weapons be partially disassembled, which may require that the objects be sent to a conservation lab for examination and condition assessment.

Display of weapons creates a security concern. Mounting the weapons to the case deck can provide a greater degree of security and allow the visitor a better view of the artifacts.

The Native American ceramic vessel should also be secured by a mount to avoid the potential of damage from vibration or tremor. Additional security should be provided to the objects by placing an alarm on the case. An audible alarm will probably suffice as the exhibit space is adjacent to a law enforcement office that is always staffed.

Intensity of light on the cased artifacts is quite low, making visibility and appreciation of the objects somewhat difficult. Artifacts in the case can safely withstand higher light intensities of up to 15 foot candles.

Dust and insect debris is visible on the case deck. Park staff indicates that the case is opened and cleaned once a year. Removal of the case glazing to access the artifacts is difficult. Curatorial housekeeping should be done on a more frequent cycle. If the exhibit function in this space is to be retained, the parks should consider acquiring a new case that allows for easier access and incorporates a silica gel compartment, artifact mounts, and gaskets.

The previous *Collection Management Plan* noted that there is no fire suppression or detection, or intrusion alarm. This situation has not been rectified. If the determination is made to retain the exhibit function for this space, a fire detection and suppression system should be installed.

If the quilt is to remain in its current location, it should be vacuumed on a regular basis, at a minimum twice a year, to avoid a build-up of dust and its associated problems. Consideration should also be given to padding the wooden rod from which the quilt hangs.

Grant Grove Visitor Center
(Note: This exhibit was changed in 2006.) The Mission 66 exhibit currently displays logging tools made primarily of iron alloys and wood. The exhibit is scheduled to be updated within the next few years. Plans call for all of the objects, with the exception of the 20-foot cross-cut saw, to be removed from exhibit and placed in storage. Photographs in the current exhibit have been

reproduced. All ferrous objects appear to have been treated with tannic acid, although no record of treatment is available.

The oil painting entitled "Man and the Big Tree" is mounted directly to the wall. The surface of the painting is soiled and marked with resinous drips. There is a small loss that appears to be the result of touching by visitors. Remedial conservation treatment is warranted if the painting is to remain on display.

As artifacts come off of exhibit, they should be placed into long-term storage. All objects should be closely examined as they are removed from exhibit and provided treatment if determined to be unstable. The saw should be cleaned and recoated with micro-crystalline wax before being returned to exhibit.

The space is currently protected with fire detection and suppression system, but no intrusion alarm system is in place.

Superintendent's Office Foyer Exhibit
Two fully-glazed, metal-framed exhibit cases are located in the superintendent's office. The cases have adjustable glass shelves supported by small clips. The door to each is keyed but does not have gaskets. There is no provision for silica gel compartments. The cases are illuminated by the ambient light in the office. Light intensity of up to 100 foot candles was measured on the upper portion of the cases, which have glazed top panels. This is too high a light level in which to exhibit most artifacts, historic photographs, or documents.

These cases house rotating exhibits that are prepared by the parks' museum staff and that change on a six-month to yearly basis. Currently the cases house Native American materials from the parks' collection. Most of the artifacts are small lithics (stone items), but a ceramic pot with a small base is also displayed. All the objects are displayed directly on the case deck and shelves; none have mounts to protect them from vibrations.

The *Collection Condition Survey* noted that light coming into the case from the ceiling lights was high and that a row of fluorescent tubes next to the case was removed to decrease the intensity. It recommended that light intensity should be further reduced if light-sensitive materials are to be displayed.

If these cases are to be used in the future to display museum objects, improvements should be made to lessen the potential for damage. Most importantly the shelves should be firmly secured so that they will not fall and shatter in the event of tremors or even normal vibration within the office. Objects such as the ceramic pot should be placed in a secure mount, as vibration could potentially cause it to tip over and break.

Consideration should be given to replacing these cases with higher quality, more attractive ones that provide a greater level of protection, security, and curatorial access. New cases should have a silica gel compartment, gasketed doors, securely-affixed shelving, glazing that filters UV light, and possibly internal illumination. Such cases could allow for the safe display of a wider range of artifacts from the parks' collection, including those made from organic material such as textiles and basketry, as well as historic paper documents and photographs.

Mineral King Ranger Station
This station currently displays a section of a tree on which inscriptions were carved by a nineteenth-century road survey crew, along with mining tools and equipment on loan from the Mineral King Preservation Society. The carved log section was recently cut out of a standing dead tree to prevent the loss of the inscriptions. It was treated with Bora-Care, a fungicide and insecticide, on the advice of an HFC conservator, prior to placement indoors. The log is currently stable with no evidence of active insect infestation; however, it should still be monitored for potential infestations. To prevent toppling in the event of tremors, the log should be affixed to the adjacent walls. The parks should consider accessioning and cataloging this tree section.

Some of the iron and iron alloy objects belonging to the Mineral King Preservation Society exhibit active corrosion. Removal of corrosion and treatment with tannic acid and/or micro-crystalline wax is warranted. Unstable wooden components of the tools should be consolidated.

A number of large pieces of equipment from local mining sites have been brought to the vicinity of the ranger station and left outside. Ownership of these pieces should be determined. If it is found that the NPS has ownership, a determination of whether to include these materials in the museum collection should be made. If accessioned, stabilization treatment would be required at some future date.

Alles Cabin

The Alles cabin is a three-room structure located along the Mineral King Road that contains many of the original furnishings belonging to the previous occupants. These furnishings, along with other associated objects, have been accessioned and cataloged. Some of the smaller artifacts have been moved to the Ash Mountain collection storage area and are in the process of being deaccessioned, with the understanding that they will be transferred to the Mineral King Preservation Society. Approximately 20 pieces of furniture remain in the cabin along with an assortment of smaller kitchen items such as glassware, cooking utensils, and china.

The furniture includes both rustic handmade pieces and store-bought manufactured pieces. Some of the mass-produced pieces have been extensively altered and repaired, presumably by the cabin occupants. The nature of the alterations has the potential to convey a compelling story of isolation, adaptation, and ingenuity. A number of the pieces are built in to the cabin. Most are wooden, but there are also a number of metal pieces including an enameled stove, icebox, pie safe, and bed, as well as one textile seat cushion.

The cabin appears to have been stabilized fairly recently. The windows are screened and have been recently re-glazed. The roof is tight and there is no evidence of leaks. Both the porch deck boards and shingles appear to have been recently replaced. Foundation work has also been done in the recent past. There is some fungal deterioration and damage from woodpeckers on the exterior cabin siding and trim. Window trim in particular is deteriorated. Wood shutters are currently stored inside and presumably are mounted on the outside during the winter.

Most of the furnishings are relatively stable and their appearance is appropriate to the historic period. There are some loose wood joints in the furniture and many of the iron ferrous elements have some degree of oxidation or rust. Mold is not evident within the building. Insect debris is present but there is no evidence of active infestation of wood-boring insects. Mouse droppings were present; however, no nests were found in the building. Curtains over the windows substantially limit the amount of light that enters the space.

Objects on open exhibit in historic structure museums like the Alles cabin require an increased level of curatorial care if they are to be preserved. This care requires a commitment of staff time to provide frequent and regular housekeeping and condition monitoring, as well as integrated pest management (IPM) activities.

The future of the cabin and its furnishings should be carefully planned and a determination made as to which of the furnishings should remain at the site. A furnishing plan and a condition survey of the furnishings should be undertaken. If the determination is made to remove museum objects from the cabin, additional museum storage space will be required.

Atwell's Sawmill Steam Engine
The steam engine is located in the ruins of Atwell's Sawmill, in close proximity to the Alles Cabin, on the Mineral King Road. The engine is incomplete; those elements that remain are made primarily of cast iron. In addition, there is some ferrous sheet metal, a wooden bull wheel, and remnants of canvas and rubber belting. The engine rests on large timbers that appear to have been treated by the application of oil.

The cast iron elements are in relatively good condition although some surfaces, particularly those in contact with the soil, exhibit pitting and active corrosion. Elements of the wooden bull wheel are extensively damaged by fungal decay and some have failed entirely. The hub has slipped off the iron shaft, resulting in a portion of the rim resting directly on the ground. The belting is highly deteriorated and only small remnants remain.

Although incomplete, this artifact can be preserved in its current location if provided with remedial treatment and cyclic maintenance. The wooden wheel will require consolidation and fungicidal treatment in the near future if it is to retain its original form. Treatment needs of the cast iron elements are not as pressing. Preservation of the remnants of the belting in an outdoor environment is probably not practicable. Documentation and placement of a sample of the belt remnants in museum storage is probably the most sensible course of action. As with all outdoor artifacts, to be effective, treatment will have to be relatively frequent and ongoing.

The *Cultural Resources Management Plan* (1982) notes that the steam engine at Atwell's Mill is in need of maintenance and is not included in the cyclical program. Hopefully this can be rectified before more elements are lost to deterioration.

Fire Management Offices Display

Fire management staff have collected and displayed a number of fire-related artifacts, documents, publications, and photographs. They are exhibited on the walls and in two display cases in the hallway adjacent to the fire management office. One case is accessed through two sliding doors at the rear and the other has double glazed doors at the front.

The artifacts are comprised of a variety of materials including wood, metal, textiles, and ceramics, as well as modern plastics and synthetic resins. The fire staff has made a good effort in saving these artifacts but thus far they are not collected, preserved, and accounted for in a systematic manner. The parks should consider adding the artifacts to the museum collection (where not private property) and thus providing systematic preservation and accountability.

If the determination is made to include some or all of these objects in the museum collection, they should be assessed for condition, and remedial conservation treatment should be undertaken as needed.

Collection Storage Facilities

Warehouse Basement

Artifacts are stored in two plywood rooms built into a corner of the warehouse basement. There is a single incandescent bulb on the ceiling of each space. One room, 13'9" x 6'2", houses both contemporary archeology-program tools and equipment, and large-sized museum objects including historic park signs. Among the archeology equipment is camping stove fuel, a highly-volatile fluid. This combination creates a serious fire hazard. The space has no fire suppression system. Removal of the volatile fluid and placement in a flammable cabinet should be done in the near future.

The second small room houses both groundstone archeological artifacts and oversized museum objects, including logging equipment, CCC era tools, and architectural elements from the Giant Forest historic buildings. There are three open shelving units along one wall and a number of artifacts placed on the floor, making access to the space difficult.

These two storage areas have no independent climate control. The spaces are not insulated, so the environment closely reflects the conditions in the warehouse space as a whole. No past environmental data is available. A dial hygrometer, lying horizontally on a storage shelf, reads 45%. An electronic hygrometer measurement at the same time read 27% RH and 81° F. Both spaces are soiled and disorganized. Loose identifying tags are found on shelves. There is evidence of rodent and insect activity.

The parks should work to move all museum artifacts from this space as more secure and environmentally-controlled space becomes available in the collections storage area. In the meanwhile, steps can be taken to significantly improve the existing space. Museum artifacts should be separated from contemporary archeology equipment. The spaces should be better organized. Artifacts should be placed on shelves in a more compact and efficient manner, providing additional shelf space so that most artifacts, including all archeological materials, can be removed from the floor. The space should be thoroughly cleaned. Sticky traps should be put out and monitored on a regular basis. The space should be sealed against rodents to the extent possible. Snap traps should be set out for rodents and checked on a frequent basis.

Central Museum Storage (Ash Mountain Headquarters Building)

The central museum storage space is on the lower level of the headquarters building. It is comprised of an outer office, darkroom, vault, and general collections area. The vault and collections area are accessed through a metal fire door with combination lock. The space does not have its own dedicated HVAC system, but is heated and cooled by the zoned building system (see Issue A).

The storage spaces have alarms for intrusion and fire with an audible alarm also connected to the park dispatch office. A fire-suppression system utilizing FM-200 gas was installed in 1996. The gas is considered to be non-ozone depleting and safe for collections and personnel. There are three heads, one in the vault and two in the general collection area, which discharge within 10 seconds of signal. The park has a contract in place to have the system inspected every six months. The inspection consists of a test of the circuitry and audible alarm system, cleaning of detectors, and a check of the pressure and liquid level of the FM-200. The fire-suppression system is designed to be effective for a closed space of a given volume. If the space changes in configuration or size, the system will need to be redesigned.

A fire-suppression system is planned for the other spaces in the Ash Mountain Headquarters building, which should provide adequate protection for portions of the collection if moved to the darkroom and curatorial workroom, as discussed in Issue A.

The vault, originally used by the Natural History Association, is accessed through a large steel and masonry door that is usually kept closed but not locked. It currently houses open shelving units, on which are stored books and film canisters, and three well-sealed museum cabinets with double doors. One cabinet houses the bulk of the basketry collection, which has been treated by WACC conservators. Custom storage enclosures have been made for each piece. The other cabinets house the remainder of the basketry along with a variety of other objects including framed artwork. Plastic containers holding documents, photographs, and computer disks are stacked on the floor and a large framed painting rests against one wall. Wooden architectural elements lie on top of two of the cabinets.

Three overhead water pipes have been wrapped and caulked, as per the recommendations of the previous CMP, to lessen the possibility of water leaks. A device that appears to be a water sensor is glued to the floor beneath the pipes and attached to telephone lines. Current museum staff has no knowledge of the purpose of this device and no information is found in the files. An alarmed water sensor is a good precaution against flooding. This device should be checked and if no longer operable, a new sensor should be installed with both an audible alarm and a connection to the dispatch office.

The central storage space houses two rows of Spacesaver™ units with an isle in the center. A map cabinet and refrigerator are located against the far wall (see Figure 2).

The key cabinet, which should be securely affixed to a wall, rests on a storage cabinet. A fire extinguisher is also not affixed to the wall as it should be. While some cabinets are up on risers, others rest directly on the floor. Unused hygrothermographs sit atop a number of cabinets.

Environmental Conditions

Environmental conditions in the space are monitored by two ACR data loggers. One has been placed in the vault and the second in the main storage space. The loggers, set up to record up to six months' of data, have not been downloaded since 2004, thus overwriting previous data. For this report, data from April 1st through September 1st 2005 was downloaded and graphed. Earlier graphs covering the time period from 12/1/03 through 5/1/04 were available. Together this data provides a reasonably good picture of the environmental conditions over the course of a year.

Accuracy of the data, however, cannot be assumed because the ten-year-old loggers lose accuracy as they age, and they have not been recalibrated since purchase. Batteries for these units are expected to last about ten years. Although the batteries can be replaced and the loggers recalibrated, it is often simpler to replace the loggers with new units.

Not surprisingly, the data indicates that the vault room is somewhat more stable in terms of temperature and RH than the central storage room, although conditions in both spaces are acceptable for mixed collections. For the five-month period from April to September, temperature in the vault ranged from 68° to 74° F with a mean of 71°. Temperature in the storage room ranged from 66° to 74° F with a mean of 69°. Relative humidity in the vault ranged from 31% to 49% with a mean RH of 43%, while in the central storage room the RH ranged from 18% to 45% with a mean of 34%. The excursion below 20% was short-lived.

Statistics are not available for the winter months, but the graphs indicate that the RH ranged from the low 30s to the low 40s. The temperature remained fairly constant with a mean of about 70° F. Both sets of graphs show a saw-tooth pattern, indicating a typical daily cycle of a 2° change in temperature and a 1.5% change in RH.

An examination of hygrothermograph charts from the early 1990s indicates that the temperature in the storage spaces was typically 72° F +/- 2 degrees and the RH fluctuated from 30% to 55%. Interpreting the charts is difficult because the multiple monthly cycles are inked on each chart. In any event, the data from the charts is similar to that from the loggers, with the exception that the earlier data indicates somewhat higher levels of RH. A return air register in the ceiling was blocked off at the suggestion of a WAAC conservator in the late 1990s. This creates a positive air pressure in the space and may account for the current lower wintertime RH.

Temperature and relative humidity conditions in the storage spaces are reasonably good for the type of collections in storage. The RH, although lower than generally recommended, slows the oxidation of the large collection of ferrous material and reduces the rate of deterioration of acidic paper. A disadvantage is that low RH can make paper more brittle and more likely to be damaged if handled. This situation can be rectified by slowly increasing the RH in a microclimate when the materials are to be handled by researchers or park staff.

Lower temperature in storage is preferable; however, a substantially lower temperature could cause the RH to rise to an unacceptably high level. It may be worthwhile to add or remove moisture from the storage space to maintain the RH within a narrower range; however, the environmental conditions should not be altered until a full year of accurate data is collected and analyzed.

The park should consider purchasing new data loggers and software. Preservation Environment Monitors (PEM) and Climate Notebook™ Software are recommended. The PEM monitor has a large memory capability and a real-time digital read-out that can alert staff to environmental conditions without the need of downloading data to a computer. These monitors also have extensive battery power and accurate sensors. The software has a number of useful metrics for interpreting the data and can accept raw data from a number of logger brands including ACR Systems. At minimum, four new loggers should be purchased; one each for the vault, central storeroom, exterior of the Ash Mountain Building, and the large case at the Foothills Visitor Center. If funds are available for additional loggers, one should be placed in the Alles cabin.

No evidence of mold was noted on either objects or surfaces in the storage space. The *Collection Condition Survey* indicates the presence of mold on some of the basketry and kitchen items from the Alles collection, but this condition has been addressed.

Integrated Pest Management

Integrated Pest Management (IPM) activities in museum spaces need additional investment. A number of sticky traps have been put out, but most are not dated and appear to have been in place for some time. There is no systematic record of the types of insects or other museum pests found. Half a dozen darkling beetles were seen under cabinets and between walls and cabinets. Mouse excrement and damage was found in a number of drawers and shelves, and a nest was found in a box of packing materials. Greater attention should be paid to protecting collections from pests.

Curatorial Housekeeping

Housekeeping in the space could be significantly improved. The floors and spaces under and around cabinets show a moderate amount of dirt. The park museum staff, with the assistance of the regional office, has developed a good *Preventive Maintenance Plan* that includes specific housekeeping tasks and the required frequency. Unfortunately the plan has not been followed due to lack of staff time. Curatorial housekeeping will be made easier when the space is made less crowded by the removal of some collection materials and all non-collection materials.

Reorganization of Space

Substantial additional space can be made available if objects are stored efficiently within the cabinetry (see especially Issue A). The collection will also benefit from a preservation perspective if like materials are stored together. While it is evident that some cabinets are carefully arranged, others store a variety of materials in a rather haphazard fashion. Currently, quite a few framed paintings, prints, and photographs are stored flat on cabinet shelves and within drawers. Additional space can be made available if these framed materials are instead hung on a painting rack or in vertical slots. Vertical storage is also preferable in terms of preservation.

The refrigerator, which houses nitrate negatives, film, and prints, is located against the far wall of the central storage room. It could be moved out and placed in the current darkroom space. Removal will free up space for a paintings rack and will likely improve environmental conditions in the space. The refrigerator compressor gives off heat, which raises the temperature in the space and reduces RH. Its removal should slightly lower the room temperature and raise the room RH.

The darkroom currently houses photo developing equipment, chemicals, a large sink, a freezer, curatorial files, and an assortment of curatorial supplies. It is overcrowded and disorganized. Actual use as a darkroom is infrequent. The park could remove the sink and photo equipment and use the space to house collections and/or supplies (see Issue A). It could also house the oversized objects currently in warehouse storage, as well as the freezer and refrigerator. A double door could be installed to make it easy to move oversized materials, but this benefit will need to be balanced against the loss of wall space.

Consideration should be given to moving the herbarium cabinets to the current office space, which could be converted to a curatorial work space. This change will allow easier access to parts of the collection by researchers and staff.

In the biological storage cabinet, wet and dry specimens are mixed together. These specimens should be separated. If not needed by the park staff, consideration should be given to removing the wet specimens entirely, through loan to a natural history museum. They are small in number, yet require highly technical skills that may or may not be present onsite.

Up to 50% of the artifact storage space could be potentially freed up by compacting storage, placing the herbarium cabinets in the curatorial workspace, and removing framed materials from the cabinets. This freed-up space could provide room for many of the artifacts currently stored in the warehouse, those objects coming off exhibit at the Grant Grove Visitor Center, and the likely addition of archival and natural history materials to the collection.

Curatorial supplies and packing materials are found in the storage room. They are no doubt located here because of lack of space in the office and the absence of a curatorial workroom. The presence of these materials clutters the storage space, creates a fire hazard, and hampers access to the collection and curatorial housekeeping. These materials should be removed as space becomes available in a curatorial workroom.

Condition Survey Needs

Paper archives and photographs comprise one of the largest components of the collection. These materials were not included in the overall survey undertaken in 1997, and they have never been examined by a conservator. A survey of these materials can check the paper and photograph environmental requirements and any treatment needs of specific items.

Remedial Conservation Needs

A preliminary sampling of the materials in storage indicates that their condition is uneven. The *Collection Condition Survey* made specific recommendations for artifact treatment. The highest priority treatments appear to have been carried out, but a considerable amount of remedial conservation treatment remains to be done. Many artifacts are soiled, and quite a few of the ferrous materials have active corrosion. It appears that some recently accessioned artifacts need cleaning and processing.

Recommendations

- Provide additional museum staff, or redirect activities of existing museum staff, to adequately address ongoing preventive conservation tasks. These tasks include curatorial housekeeping, pest management, and environmental monitoring. Implement the existing *SEKI Preventive Maintenance Plan*. If inadequate staff time is available, prioritize tasks and track accomplishments to allow for an assessment of their effectiveness.

- Reorganize warehouse storage rooms. Remove volatile fluids from warehouse storage areas. Segregate museum artifacts from tools and equipment. Remove all organic and high-value artifacts. Move all possible items off the floor and place on either shelves or pallets. Remove all museum objects from the warehouse storage areas and place in the collections storage building as space becomes available.

- Reorganize central collection storage areas. Remove the darkroom function and convert the darkroom space to storage of oversized objects. Consolidate artifacts within cabinets and store like objects together.

- Relocate offices from current office space and convert it to curatorial workspace. Move curatorial supplies from storage area and place in curatorial workspace. Move herbarium collection and place in curatorial workspace.

- Analyze environmental conditions at the Ash Mountain central museum storage space after the collection of accurate environmental data covering a full year. Improve environmental conditions as recommended.

- Conduct a survey of paper and photographic materials.

- Continue the remedial conservation treatment of artifacts as recommended in the *Collection Condition Survey* undertaken by WAAC in 1997.

- Undertake planning of Alles Cabin furnishings. Assess the collection for preservation needs and determine what can remain on exhibit and what needs to be placed into storage.

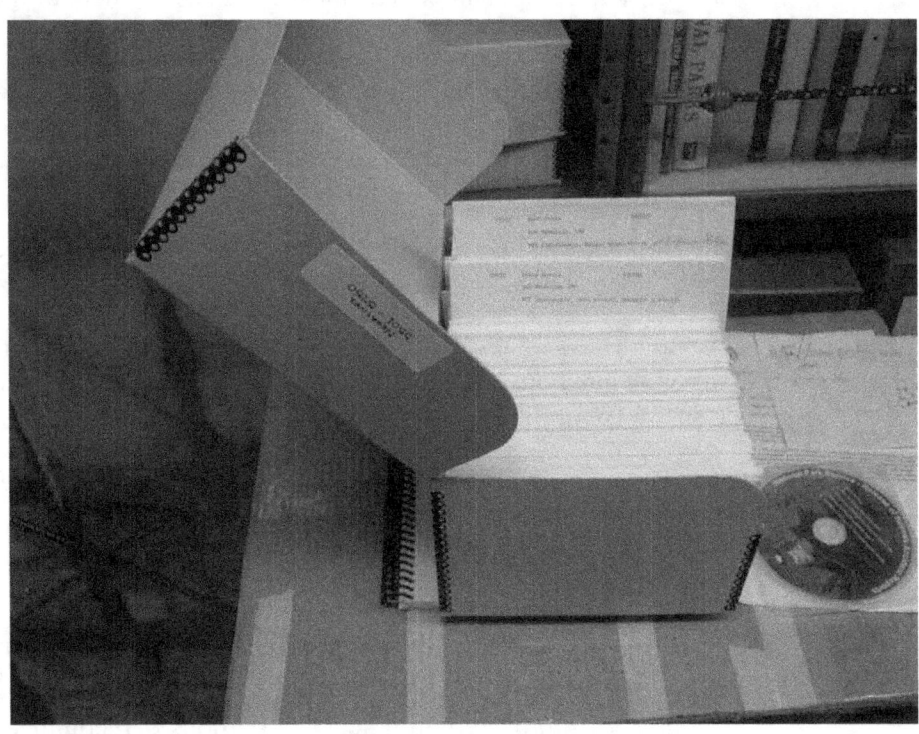

Figure 6 Photo sleeves in flip-top box within SEKI archives.

Issue Statement

Successful management of park archives requires their professional reorganization and arrangement with upgraded storage and workspace to meet the needs of growth, research, and park program support.

Background

Sequoia and Kings Canyon National Parks have a valuable archive collection which is instrumental for the successful day-to-day operations at the parks. The parks have consistently maintained their museum program by staffing museum positions and keeping the museum collection in proper storage. Currently, archive collections are located in the central museum storage of the Ash Mountain Headquarters building.

The park archives are comprised predominantly of resource management records, which are official records needed for ongoing management of resources at the parks. This is typical of NPS archive collections. The parks also have a few manuscript collections, which are personal papers donated from non-NPS sources. There are also some fragmented collections, which would best be described as ephemera.

The archives program is currently challenged by a space shortage. According to the *SEKI Collection Management Report* (2004), the archives currently house 300,637 items or 188 linear feet (LF) of accessioned and non-accessioned documents, flat files, and photos. However, there are an estimated 150 LF of archives and roughly 600 maps, plans, and drawings located in storage and offices throughout the parks that need to be accessioned into the museum archives. The current available archives storage would be hard-pressed to house these additional materials.

There is also no dedicated space to store pre-accessioned materials, to process archival collections, or to allow researchers secure space for access and reference. Currently, these activities occur in the office space of cultural resources located just outside the central storage. As a result of this arrangement, newly-arrived museum collections are not correctly housed and are exposed to risk elements such as food, beverages, biological and rodent infestation, potential theft, and inadvertent damage.

For the archives program to move forward, a critical flaw in the arrangement of the archives first needs to be resolved. The park museum program has lacked the fulltime professional services of a trained archivist. Prior to the 1980s, the parks stored their official records at the Federal Records Center (FRC) in San Bruno. The parks had these records returned, and many of these documents were accessioned into the archives as resource management records.

The records from San Bruno were mixed with the official records stored at the parks, and together these formed the "park files," which constitute the bulk of the archives at the parks. However, during the creation of the park files, the collection was not arranged or described by an archivist, but rather was placed, with no logical order, into boxes that were numbered sequentially. As a result, the original order of the collections was not kept intact, and provenance from creating divisions has been blurred, if not erased.

To further complicate the integrity of the collection, ongoing accretions have been added to the collection, which inherently makes this an open collection, and thereby forces all additional accretions to retain the flawed structure of the original collection. The parks currently rely on box and folder lists for access and employ a database to search keywords.

To correct this system, the park files collection needs to be arranged and described by a professional archivist and cataloged into the Automated National Catalog System version 2 (ANCS+) archives module. In addition, a finding aid needs to be produced. These steps will greatly increase accessibility and allow future park records to retain their integrity when added to the archives.

The first park archives survey was conducted in 1985 by private contractor Waverly B. Lowell. This was an in-depth survey that provided accurate archival guidance and examined each division, covering most record locations in the parks at that time. The parks followed up by implementing the majority of the survey's recommendations. The parks successfully acquired records into the museum collection archives and processed the records in accordance with professional guidelines.

Lowell referred to the original system of the park file collection in recommending that the parks "re-establish the central file system." In addition, she recommended moving library materials out of the museum vault and into the library, and moving subject files, theses, dissertations, and other archival materials from the library to the archives. These recommendations have not yet been fully implemented. Although many of the recommendations are no longer relevant, the survey is now a definitive source of provenance for many records that previously arrived into the park archives, and it may prove useful in any future re-organizing of the parks' archive collections into organic record groups. Lowell's recommendations on motion picture film, managing the library, and procedures for processing collections remain accurate.

A Collection Management Plan (CMP) was produced at the parks in 1992 and finalized in 1997. NPS Archivist Lynn Marie Mitchell wrote the archives chapter for this CMP. Mitchell provided detailed guidance on the manuscript collections and on preserving the integrity of collections by curtailing the practice of allowing open collections. This recommendation has still not been implemented by the parks. She also identified specific documentation in the maintenance office and library that needed to be accessioned into the archives. Many of these materials still need to be acquired. Mitchell also found some nitrates and potential di-acetates and recommended a more extensive review of the photograph collections to sequester and properly store these potentially hazardous materials.

Several of her recommendations have not yet been fully implemented by the parks. These include:

- Acquiring identified park files for inclusion into the park archives.

- Bringing in a professional archivist to help resolve some of the fundamental problems with the collections.

- Producing finding aids.

- Ending the practice of open-ended collections.

In July 1998, a second archives and records survey was completed at SEKI by NPS Archivist Lisbit Bailey. This survey provides an overview of archival management and provides detailed instructions on preserving specific items in the archives (most of which are still applicable, such as reformatting, making use-copies, and stabilizing the CCC scrapbooks). Bailey's survey reinforced several of the issues and recommendations from Lowell's survey, and relies on that survey for locations of active, semi-active and inactive records within the parks.

The 1998 survey also revealed a few new developments, such as power blackouts and brownouts, that affect the museum. If power issues are still a recurring problem, the parks will need to investigate the use of an emergency backup, such as a generator or at least an uninterruptible power supply. The survey also suggests sending the freezer and nitrates from the park archives to WACC or SAFR for storage. Bailey reinforces the need for additional researcher space, workspace, and storage space. In addition, the survey provides suggested steps for processing and preservation of collections, and it includes current guidance on the management of the parks' library system. The parks have implemented a few of her recommendations, but a large percentage still remain to be implemented by the parks.

Discussion

The parks' dedicated museum collection storage space is inadequate to house all the archive collections within the parks without major modifications. Archival materials that should be accessioned and processed into the collection remain in substandard conditions in the warehouse, trailers, attic, floor space, and filing cabinets in offices. There is simply not enough room left in the museum storage to add in these additional materials without substantial reorganization of space (see Issue A).

The storage of inactive records in the warehouse is a necessary tool to manage park official records, but the parks will need to acquire space that has better environmental controls and is more defensible against biological and rodent infestation. There are approximately 150 linear feet of archival records in storage or in active use at the parks. There are also over 500 maps, plans, and drawings that are in active use but are also archival. These should be acquired into the museum collections in the near future so that they can be preserved and protected. Plans and drawings that have not yet been sent to the Technical Information Center in Denver, Colorado need to be sent so that they can be microfilmed and digitized.

The parks need additional room for museum and archive processing and dedicated reference workspace. Ideally, these locations should be kept delineated so that materials being processed are protected from access by researchers (i.e., touching, spilling, and theft). The current arrangement combines museum office workspace, museum processing space, and research reference space into one small room. This space is woefully inadequate and will require corrective measures.

The complex nature of the SEKI collections requires a museum professional to manage these collections. The bulk of the collections at SEKI are archival and a large majority of research requests at the parks are for access to archival collections, so the parks should consider creating a professional archivist position in addition to the current museum technician position. The parks have placed large responsibilities on their museum technician, with emphasis on managing the archives, museum collections, and libraries, and on providing assistance with records management and historical research at the parks. With an investment in training and guidance, the museum technician should be able to more effectively manage the program. However, the needs of the museum program suggest that at least two positions with the skill sets of multiple specialists will be needed. One person alone, especially at the technician level, will continue to be challenged to successfully manage the entire SEKI museum program.

Outreach

The park museum program receives about 100 formal research requests per year, 50 of which are in-house staff requests. Of these 100 requests, about 95 are for access to archival collections. The museum, archives, and library collections survey completed by 30 staff members at SEKI revealed that 80% of the respondents used the park archives over 200 times last year. Highest use collections as determined by park respondents included photo collections (67%), natural resource records (63%), and administrative records (63%). The primary reason given for archive use was to "address internal NPS needs."

Section III of the survey reveals that 60% of respondents wanted increased accessibility from either electronic means or a listing/finding aid of what is in the archives. It is apparent that everyone will benefit from better access to the archive collections. However, some substantial tasks need to be completed to support optimized access to the collections. The parks need to resolve the lack of adequate work and research space, reorganize the archives collection, and catalog the remainder of the archives backlog. Until these issues are resolved, gaining access to the museum collections will be time-consuming and inconsistent. Once this work has been finished, outreach, reference, and access to the collections will be much more efficient.

Records Management

In the last few decades, records management has become a crucial issue at many parks. The park's administrative officer is ultimately responsible for official records at the park, but often there are no day-to-day "records managers" at parks, and these duties are largely collateral. Currently, the park's 'mail and files' clerk within Administration is responsible for the management of central files in the park. The parks will need to assess the effectiveness of its records management. This task will become even more critical with regards to the increasing prevalence of electronic records. In order for the NPS central files system to be effective, it relies on the creator of records to enter the correct central file code. Incorrect coding can lead to erroneous dispositions of potentially critical records. *Director's Order#19 (DO#19)* has been superseded in the last year by a newer version that identifies "resource management records" that are to be archived at the parks. Sequoia and Kings Canyon National Parks, like most parks, are working to adapt to these new program changes.

While the central file system is an effective tool for managing park administrative records, NPS archivists and records managers have recently advised park divisions to begin implementing a "project checklist" approach to managing records. Instead of assigning central file codes to all documents, the project checklist relies on the creators of project files to keep the project intact and label the files in such a way that they are clearly tied to an over-arching project. Examples of project checklists are included in Appendix C. Managing records as projects can be much more effective, and once inactive, these collections are easier to appraise and make accessible once accessioned into the park archives.

Inactive park records are predominantly stored in the Maintenance warehouse. These records are kept locked and there is plenty of room for their storage. However, as a fair percentage of these records are archival, issues such as security, preservation, and organization become a greater concern. The warehouse storage space does not have adequate environmental controls, and there is visible evidence of biological and rodent infestation. There are currently seven filing cabinets with central files from the 1980s and 1990s. Also in the storage area are boxes of budget, fiscal, and resource management records (RMR). RMR are archival, and examples that can be found in this area include two boxes of DEPO administrative files, burn files, contract documentation, and two boxes upstairs with central file codes "Y" and "W."

Of perhaps even greater concern are the records stored in metal trailers by the Natural Resources division. Photos, slides, cassettes, electronic media, and paper documentation deteriorate at an exponentially faster rate in such rudimentary storage. Not only will the heat and fluctuating humidity cut the lifespan of this documentation by 75%, the off-gassing of certain mediums, such as diazos, will also accelerate the deterioration of otherwise stable formats. As there are archival resource management records in these trailers, it is imperative that the parks locate more optimal temporary storage. The cost to replace this baseline documentation is far greater then the cost of temporary storage.

Periodically, the museum technician collects inactive records from storage in the warehouse for acquisition into the archives. Often this is done at the suggestion of subject specialists that recognize the value of certain records. If the parks are ever in doubt about the appraisal of record disposition (whether a record should be retained or disposed), they should consult with an NPS archivist before making the final determination.

To resolve these complex issues, the parks will need to designate a team of park staff to manage and monitor electronic and records management issues at the parks. There is guidance available to help the parks with guidelines, standards, and policies. The parks will also need to be vigilant in safeguarding electronic records.

Metadata (the data that explains where data came from, and its organization and history) can be lost with serious harm done to existing databases. Some data and metadata can be made unusable once printed to hardcopy (for example, complex images in GIS maps, graphics, and videos). The parks need to develop a policy for managing and migrating analog and digital files and databases (with accompanying data and metadata). For the parks to be truly effective in this endeavor, park staff needs to receive necessary training and a commitment from park management to support records management policies and procedures. If these procedures are not followed, the cost to retrieve information from obsolescent technology eventually becomes astronomical and critical baseline data and institutional history will disappear. The long-term objective for the parks should be to focus less on having a single records manager and more on having each individual staff member be responsible for their own records.

SOPs and Protocols

A professional museum program relies on creating and implementing standard operating procedures (SOPs) and protocols. Examples of these include "Access and Use," "Copyright and Privacy Restrictions," "Migration and Reformatting Procedures," and so on. In addition to housekeeping plans, Integrated Pest Management plans, and Emergency Operations Procedures, these guidelines are vital tools that provide a framework for everyday operations. However, these tools need to be kept current, and more importantly, be followed by the museum program. Included in Appendix B is an example of an Access and Use policy from Pipe Springs National

Monument that can be used as an example to help direct the current SEKI Access and Use policy.

PMIS Projects

The SEKI archives need a backlog-cataloging (BACCAT) project and a paper and photo Collection Condition Survey (CCS). The current workload on the lone SEKI museum technician is more than one entry-level position can manage. As a result, some tasks are not being completed, which translates into a backlog of work. There are roughly 150 LF of records in storage waiting to be acquired into the archives and to be preserved and cataloged. This work is equivalent to one position working for three years. In addition, SEKI serves as a repository for Devils Postpile National Monument (DEPO) museum collections. Some of the DEPO collections are also backlogged.

As of 2005, all documents created prior to 1999 are eligible for backlog-cataloging funding (previously, it had been prior to 1987). SEKI could submit a backlog-cataloging project requesting funding for three years, and include a component for cataloging the DEPO archives. The project could request $40,000 a year, for a three-year total of $120,000, to obtain professional archival services for this work.

The parks should also submit an MCPPP Project Management Information System (PMIS) project to have a paper and photo CCS conducted by a conservator, with subject matter expertise in these formats. A CCS project typically costs between $7,000 and $12,000.

The SEKI archives also need the professional assistance of an archivist to reorganize the park files. As this collection has already been cataloged (although to a substandard level), the parks are not eligible to receive BACCAT funding for this work. In reality, the collection has not been cataloged; it simply has a box and folder list. It is suggested that the parks contact the regional curator to inform her of this situation and ask her guidance on how best to resolve this issue. This project qualifies for Cultural Resource Preservation Program funds and would rate highly against the program's criteria. It is recommended that a team of NPS archivists be brought in to quickly establish the hierarchy, and arrange and describe the collections. The team could also assist the parks in accessioning new materials as distinct record groups or collections.

ANCS+

A quick review of the archive collections in ANCS+ revealed the following four problems. These problems need to be corrected to allow further archival processing to proceed without obstacles.

1. DEPO accessions have been listed in and with SEKI accessions. Although SEKI is serving as the repository for DEPO collections, DEPO accessions need to be managed in a designated DEPO accessions directory.

2. A few of the allocated SEKI accession numbers have not been entered into the SEKI accessions directory.

3. Previous archival items cataloged into ANCS+ have been entered incorrectly. Numerous photos, videocassettes, maps, reports, and newspapers have been entered as history objects in the classification field and not classified as archives. At some point the parks might consider updating these classifications so that entries are consistently classified.

4. The majority of the archives collections have not yet been imported or cataloged into the archives module of ANCS+. For these archival collections to be fully accessed and managed (and as part of all future cataloging work), they should be cataloged to the folder level—and in certain instances, the item level—in the archives module.

Park Collections

The condition of archives is, overall, in very good condition. The park files collection has a mix of early decimal-coded files and central file codes. This collection has no established hierarchy or series, and it has not been arranged or described. The integrity of the collections has been eroded and the original order is no longer intact. "Collections" and "Manuscripts" have been given two-letter alpha designations. In addition, there are other types of designations such as "CD" for cataloged documents. This alpha-coding is somewhat cryptic and not intuitive, but most importantly, it does not meet archival standards. This system and practice must be eliminated.

Archival collections originating from the parks should be placed into discreet record groups with titles such as "SEKI Interpretive Files 1922-1948." Later accretions would be evidenced by a distinct date range. The parks have applied the literal translation of "manuscripts" to five previously accessioned collections and have removed some manuscript materials from the park files. In order to preserve original order, this practice must be eliminated. Currently, the manuscript collection would more ideally function as the appropriate place to house personal papers acquired from non-NPS sources. With a sizeable amount of ephemera (such as pamphlets, clippings, items without provenance, and ribbons) the parks should create a distinct collection of these materials.

Also, some documentation in the archives would be more appropriately designated as reference or vertical files. A reference collection or vertical file could be developed in close proximity to the library so that all staff would have access to it.

The archives have some preservation concerns; rolled plans and drawings need to be relaxed by a conservator. Certain files and documents within archival document boxes are falling over or slouching; these will need to have buffered spacers placed into the boxes to prevent this. Some of the scrapbooks have had pages encapsulated. Although this is a good intention to try to preserve these materials, the scrapbook pages are highly acidic and the encapsulation creates a micro-climate that accelerates the deterioration. Collections storage needs additional flat file storage for maps, plans, and drawings (roughly twice the amount of current storage) to accommodate the materials in the parks that need to be accessioned into the archives.

Located within the audio visual room (adjacent to the central museum storage) are items that can be accessioned into the archives and reformatted. These materials include motion picture film, oral history audio cassettes from the 1970s, videotapes, and 100 reel-to-reel audio tapes dating from the 1960s. These formats will need to be migrated in order to remain accessible and preserved (the reel-to-reels are already in a stable media and should be archived, but they should also be digitized so that they are readily accessible).

Future Archives
The list below includes offices that were surveyed for resource management records and a brief description of materials located at these sites:

- **Natural Resources (NR):** Active and semi-active collections are located in a gray zircon trailer in front of the NR building; flat files inside the Headquarters office building; and a 1950s Airstream™ travel trailer at the Natural Resources (NR) building on Sycamore Street. In addition, the Cave files located on the top floor of the Fire Management office will also be an extremely valuable, archival collection, once they are considered inactive.

- **Fire Management:** The attic space has a set of archival oversized material, several containers of archival slides, and a few boxes of potential archival records.

- **Concessions:** The land and project files are resource management records and archival. These are located within filing cabinets in this office.

- **Warehouse storage:** Central files storage contains temporary and permanent records. There are also two boxes in the lower level of the warehouse with Concession and Interpretation resource management records.

- **GIS:** Aerials, maps, and other primary documentation are located in this office.

- **Resource Management:** A large amount of historic files is located in filing cabinets in the central Resource Management office.

- **Administration:** Projects, General Management Plan, contracts, and current central files. Much of these are resource management records and will be archival.

- **Maintenance Offices:** Flat files, contracts, material safety data sheets, building files, completion reports, etc., are located within the main Maintenance office. Most of these are resource management records and many of the flat files will need to be sent to the Technical Information Center to be microfilmed.

- **Library:** Materials identified in previous surveys. The parks have done a good job managing the library, which has most of the holdings posted on the network.

Recommendations

- Create additional storage space to adequately house the museum collections and inactive park records (see Issue A). Create museum processing space and researcher reference space.

- Provide training for the museum technician with formal professional workshops, informal details, or detail opportunities at other parks.

- Create a professional GS-11 Archivist position to manage the parks' museum and records program. This may initially be a three-year term position until base funding can be obtained.

- Reorganize existing archival collections. This requires professional arrangement and description, cataloging into the ANCS+ archives module, and production of finding aids.

- Create an accession of inactive archival records from warehouse and offices. Submit a PMIS project to complete this work.

- Implement a park-wide records and electronic records management program using a team approach. Delineate responsibility for managing the records program.

- Develop and implement protocols and standard operating procedures for managing a professional museum and archive program.

Figure 7 Accession book and records in file drawer.

Issue D — Museum Records

Issue Statement

The parks seek to achieve thorough and professional documentation of the ownership and history of their museum and archive collections to maximize their value to all potential users.

Background

National Park Service (NPS) museum records document park ownership and legal custody of museum objects and archives, and they identify, describe, and evaluate collections. The research value of collections derives largely from such records. As one of the older museum collections in the NPS, Sequoia and Kings Canyon National Parks' records reflect the history of museum documentation within the NPS and record an important collection of museum property.

SEKI's earliest accession of museum property dates to 1926. The National Park Service's requirements, as well as the standards of the greater museum community, have changed profoundly since that time. The types of records kept, and even the types of property included in the parks' collection, have changed in the intervening years. Unlike other park records, museum records are permanent, and they need to be updated to current standards to allow for optimal access to information about the resources in the collection and for their proper preservation and use. Improvement of SEKI's records will improve accountability for the parks' collection and increase its value for research and exhibition.

Discussion

Documentation of Unprocessed Materials

There is a large volume of unaccessioned material at SEKI, which is a significant management concern. This lack of documentation causes accountability problems, affects the utility of the collection, and affects the projections for museum space storage needs. Materials turned in to SEKI museum staff for addition to the collection have not been promptly assessed or processed. This is an accountability problem in itself, but may also result in loss of the associated information for these objects and a loss of value to the parks as a result. Undocumented collections cannot be properly inventoried, treated, or accessed for research.

During the Museum Management Plan site visit, many unaccessioned materials were noted in the collection storage area, office space, and darkroom. Some materials were partially labeled or identified, but others seemed to have no associated identifying information. The notes that were found included both undated and dated information, including one case dated twelve years earlier. An unaccessioned firearm was found in the fireproof filing cabinet behind the accession files (see Figure 7).

The bulk of this material suggests it may represent well over 100 accessions. This problem is related to limited staff, but it is also exacerbated by inadequate space for examining and processing collections. A discrete area to store unprocessed collections is optimal, but in any case, clear labeling and inventory are essential to preserve documentation for collections being considered for acquisition, as well as for accessioned collections awaiting further processing or cataloging. No materials should be accepted for potential evaluation and assessment without complete written information containing the relevant who, where, why, and when of the collection.

Training

Museum recordkeeping is a specialized topic. In the past, training was available to most NPS staff with collections responsibilities. Although these opportunities have dwindled, details at parks with larger museum programs provide another option to gain these skills. The museum technician at SEKI has had no training in museum recordkeeping and would benefit from greater knowledge of NPS policies and procedures. Many national parks in California have well-established museum programs, and these programs present an opportunity to obtain this training at minimal expense to SEKI. Staff from other parks, such as Yosemite (also a part of the Sierra Network), can offer consultation and assistance on museum recordkeeping.

Accession Book and Accession Files

The SEKI accession book and files were reviewed as part of this planning effort. They need some corrective work to meet NPS standards for documenting ownership of collections and to help maximize the value of collections for research. Examples of problematic accession book entries include those that:

- Have been made in pencil (SEKI-1044).

- Lack dates (SEKI-1054).

- Lack accession type (SEKI-1044).

- Lack quantification (SEKI-1060).

- Lack source information (SEKI-1049).

Meeting professional documentation standards is essential to effective resource management, as demonstrated during the team's visit by the discovery of unclear title to materials that are being considered for a North American Graves Protection and Repatriation Act (NAGPRA) deaccession action (SEKI-120). As critical primary documentation of the collection, both the accession book and all accession files should all be stored inside the vault. With these files quite active, the blue four-drawer filing cabinet near the vault door would be a good place to keep them. Other less frequently used records, such as DEPO accession files and back-up hard copies of catalog records, could be moved to the fireproof file on the Spacesaver™ carriage.

The accession files also need to provide a better level of documentation for incoming material. Inappropriate and unrelated materials were found in these files, and other necessary or useful documents were missing. These files should be reviewed for missing documentation, and other files in the museum office, which might relate to incoming accessions or other museum actions such as loans and deaccessions, should be reviewed. Related materials should be copied on archival paper and added to the accession files. Important notes originally made on acidic paper should be copied onto archival paper for these permanent records (see SEKI-1065).

Photographs related to accessions should ordinarily be stored outside the fireproof files, as these do not provide optimal storage for photographs, but they should be stored together and clearly marked with accession numbers. A cross-reference to the existence of photographs and/or photocopies, which includes information on their format and location, should be placed in appropriate accession files.

ANCS+ Database

Since 1987, NPS museum records have been incorporated into a computerized Automated National Cataloging System (ANCS). In its current form (ANCS+), this software also manages accession, inventory, and facilities data important to collection management, access, and funding. Nearly 16,000 catalog records and over 1,050 accession records from SEKI have been entered into this system.

As SEKI depends on these databases for collection access, and the regional office and Washington Support Office (WASO) increasingly use these databases to monitor work and progress within park collections and to determine eligibility for funding, it is critical that these records be maintained and kept up-to-date. Apparently, because data was not supplied to WASO with the record submission, the 2004 collection management report shows no loans, no exhibits, and no research use of SEKI's collection. Currently, DEPO records are mixed into the SEKI database. Additionally, at least 29 SEKI accession records are not included in the database, including accessions for 2003 through 2005. These omissions result in incorrect annual collection management report submissions.

The past nine years of collection management reports were reviewed for collections activity, and the results are shown in Table 2 and graphed in Figure 8. These reports indicate an annual growth rate of approximately 1% and a substantial reduction in the backlog of uncataloged materials (or backlog). Of course, this does not include unprocessed material currently in museum custody, as discussed here and in Issue C. As this material is processed, an increase in these figures can be anticipated.

Date	Backlog	Cataloged Collection	Total Museum Holdings
2004	5,710	339,160	344,870
2003	5,710	339,160	344,870
2002	2,498	339,160	341,658
2001	2,824	335,924	338,748
2000	68,837	251,149	319,986
1999	80,704	239,000	319,704
1998	70,363	238,830	309,193
1997	70,434	238,265	308,699

Table 2 Growth of museum collections at Sequoia and Kings Canyon National Parks

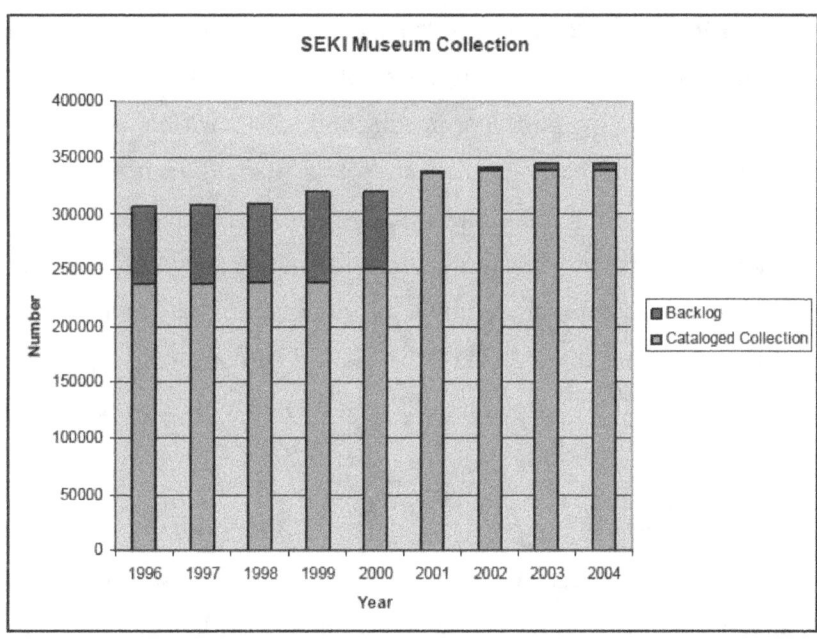

Figure 8 Growth of SEKI museum collection (1996-2004)

Written Park-Specific Procedures

Developing standard operating procedures (SOP) for the SEKI museum and archive collection would serve as a guide for park staff and provide consistency in collections care. These SOPs would include:

- Operating hours
- Points of contact (staff phone numbers and email addresses)
- Notice required for research appointments
- Types of access permitted
- Procedures for ordering duplicates from the collection
- General information on loans from the collection
- Guidelines on handling of field-collected material
- Information on accessioning guidelines and procedures

The SOPs would provide a written record of guidelines and expectations understood by current staff members, and they would assist museum staff in maintaining a consistent program. Developed by park staff and approved by the park superintendent, SOPs establish a set of formal policies for the museum program to operate by.

Inventory / Outgoing Loan / Deaccession Records

Outgoing loans from the museum collection must be formalized and documented using NPS loan forms, and they must be recorded in the ANCS+ database. Some loan records were found filed adjacent to the accession files, but none were entered in the database. Other loans of park property are known to museum staff (e.g., herbarium specimens at Duke University), but have not been documented by a loan agreement between SEKI and the repository. Current and past loans should be numbered and added to this database to improve accountability and to provide a vital record of collections activity.

Finally, in considering records, only one of the three required annual inventories has been submitted for SEKI for the past nine years. The last inventory of controlled property was submitted in 1996. A check of the ANCS database for controlled property revealed that numerous deaccessioned NAGPRA items are incorrectly listed as controlled property.

These errors need to be corrected before the inventory is completed again. No record was found of a random inventory of accessions submission. The controlled property inventory, which includes property on exhibit as well as particularly valuable holdings designated as controlled property, is particularly critical for accountability. The random inventory of accessions is also an important reflection of how well SEKI has maintained uncataloged materials. The parks should maintain the original signed copies of all inventories for at least five years. These are important records for collections management, so the museum program may opt to keep older inventories on hand indefinitely.

SEKI is in the process of deaccessioning a large collection of out-of-scope material from the museum collection. Although this can be a time-consuming process, unneeded collections use valuable storage space, staff time, and other park resources, and should therefore be removed from the parks' holdings. As this process can be controversial, the parks should carefully follow established written policy and procedures for deaccession decisions and prepare associated documentation with peer and regional input. They should secure written approval of actions at the regional level for materials that will not remain within the NPS. Separate folders for deaccession actions should be set up to compile all documentation and approvals for them. Corresponding entries should be made in the ANCS+ database to ensure that deaccessions can be tracked within the software program as well.

Accession Committee

To assist the museum technician in making accessioning determinations on materials offered to the collection and to provide an additional level of oversight for deaccession actions, SEKI should consider forming an accessions committee. Committee members could include staff from other park divisions, as well as the SEKI curator-of-record. For difficult or complex accession decisions, the regional curator or another park museum expert can be called upon for advice and consent. Members would provide input on what types of materials to add to the museum collection, guided by SEKI's Scope of Collection Statement. Members would also review material and justifications for proposed deaccessions. An added benefit of this committee is that it will raise the visibility of the museum operation within the parks by involving staff from other divisions, and it should strengthen support for the program.

DEPO Museum Records and Collections Management

SEKI currently has recordkeeping responsibilities for Devils Postpile National Monument (DEPO) museum collections and provides some storage for these collections. The scope of these duties should be specified in a memorandum of understanding or other instrument between the parks, and it should be documented in the SEKI museum technician's position description. Original DEPO accession files and the DEPO accession book are currently stored in the SEKI museum vault, and the records are incorporated in the ANCS databases for SEKI. These records should be kept in separate directories to allow independent access for management and reporting.

Backlog Cataloging / Improvement of Existing Catalog Records

As backlog accessioning is completed, an additional backlog of uncataloged material will be created. Quantifying this material will be important in obtaining future funding, identifying storage needs, and planning. Processing this backlog will improve accountability and make collections available for research and interpretive use. Additionally, work on improving existing older and less complete catalog records will enhance their value to the parks and to outside researchers.

Research Use

The museum program would benefit from the development of research policies, particularly for outside (non-NPS) researchers. Written guidelines for access and copyright/use agreements will help provide improved accountability and more accurate use statistics, as well as ensure proper handling and preservation of the museum collection. All researchers should be required to sign in and identify themselves. Information on researchers should be maintained, for security reasons, to provide more accurate use statistics, and to promote collaboration on related research projects by NPS staff and outside researchers.

Recommendations

- Pursue opportunities for additional training in museum documentation for the museum technician. Training may be courses or details at other parks or museums, although note that NPS documentation methods are unique to the agency, and thus outside museums can provide only a broader knowledge base of professional standards.

- Fully document incoming material as it is received. All field collections must have a signed receipt for property by the park staff member delivering the items.

- Review all material in museum storage and work areas to identify unprocessed or undocumented material. Review material and make determinations on whether to accession or make alternative dispositions.

- Complete accession records to NPS standards at time of accessioning.

- Review accession book and files to complete documentation for past accessions and remove inappropriate material from files.

- Complete ANCS+ database for accessions and other museum actions (loans, deaccessions, and inventory) to bring it up-to-date and produce accurate reports.

- Complete documentation for all loans, recording them in both ANCS and in files as described in the *NPS Museum Handbook*.

- Document all deaccessions following the procedures described in the *NPS Museum Handbook*. Add deaccession information to the ANCS database to reflect past and current actions.

- Write standard operating procedures (SOPs) for the SEKI museum program to establish guidelines for staff on access, acquisitions, and operations.

- Create an accessions committee to establish procedures and to review materials both for acceptance into the museum collection and for removal from the collection by deaccession.

- Formalize the relationship between DEPO and SEKI related to museum recordkeeping responsibilities by using a written agreement, and document this in the museum technician's position description and duties.

- Continue museum cataloging to address the backlog of the large quantity of poorly-documented collections and to improve the accountability and value of the holdings.

- Complete all three required annual inventories annually. File each year's set of inventories for long-term retention.

- Upgrade inadequate older catalog records.

- Write collections access policy and use agreements for use by outside researchers.

Figure 9   Butterfly and moth specimens in SEKI museum collection.

Issue Statement

The growth of the museum program and its collections is strongly linked, and each requires continued investment to meet the needs of the parks and achieve the high standards set by the National Park Service.

Background

The museum and archival collections of Sequoia and Kings Canyon National Parks reflect a hundred years of park history (see previous History of Museum Collections). They represent a valuable resource with a high informational value, as described in Issue C. Their storage, organization, documentation, and preservation, as discussed in other issues in this plan, are a component of the overall mission of the parks. This issue looks at the future of the collections and the program, and the growth that will inevitably challenge the parks to meet needs for expansion and staff capabilities, and the ability to achieve the standards necessary of parks that strive to professionally manage museum collections.

The Scope of Collection Statement (SOCS) establishes the context for the acquisition of museum collections and sets forth priorities for the growth of the collections. The current draft SOCS is contained, in part, in Appendix D. It contains the sections of the SOCS most concerned with describing the various disciplines and the logic and direction of their growth.

Growth of the Museum Collections

The latest Collections Management Report (2004) shows that the current park collection contains some 345,000 objects and records (see Table 3). Archives represent the largest segment of the collection by count, and using a conversion factor of 1,600 pages per linear feet, this would occupy some 188 linear feet of shelf space. Archeology, history, and biology are roughly equal components of the collection. Ethnology, paleontology, and geology are quite small in size, but important nevertheless.

Discipline	Cataloged	Catalog Backlog	Total
Archeology	17,813	233	18,046
Ethnology	32	0	32
History	13,543	1,827	15,370
Archives	297,197	3,440	300,637
Biology	10,255	200	10,455
Paleontology	22	0	22
Geology	298	10	308
Totals:	339,160	5,710	344,870

Table 3   SEKI museum collection size by discipline and catalog status

This plan looked at the growth of collections in a variety of ways and from the point of view of different program requirements, such as storage, processing space, and museum documentation. Growth totals for recent years are shown in Figure 8. More detailed analyses can be performed to assess past growth to assist in predicting future growth.

A review of the museum database (ANCS+) for Natural History Collections generated the chart shown in Figure 10, showing the numbers of specimens collected over time, with a few specimens collected in 1924. As mentioned in the History of Collection Management section of this plan, the database doesn't reflect the 4,000 specimens that were lost to fire in 1917. The chart in Figure 10 reflects a modest collection developing by the 1940s. A decade followed with few new additions. By the 1960s larger numbers were being collected and preserved, and after a slowdown in the mid-1970s, the sampling and collecting activities continued with ups and downs to the present day. Other specimens during this period were probably collected, but they were lost for various reasons, such as being consumed by pests, accidental mishandling, lack of documentation, or poor storage.

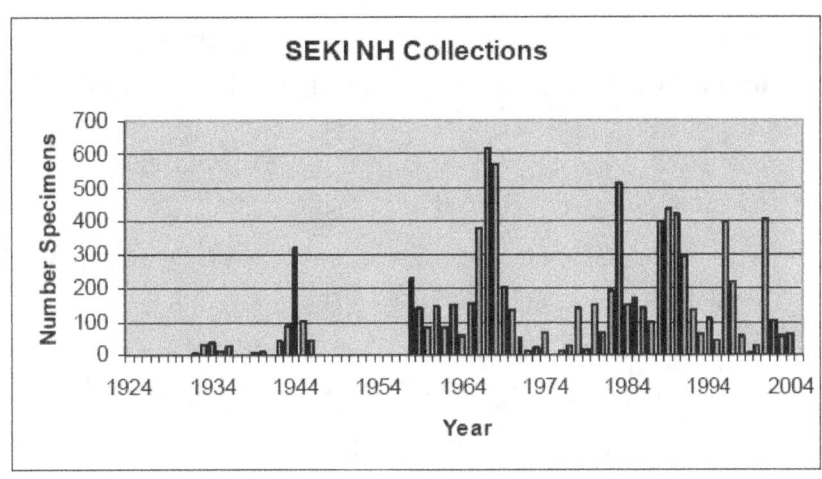

SEKI NH Collections

Figure 10 Number of SEKI natural history specimens collected over time as documented in ANCS+.

Although the ANCS+ database does not reflect the parks' collections that were transferred to outside colleges and universities, it does provide a view of collecting activities and the time-range coverage of the specimens. A general conclusion from Figure 10 is that the collection of park biological specimens has been a long-term and fairly steady priority for the parks. With the recent development of the Inventory and Monitoring program and the growth of other natural resource programs, these collections will continue to grow in the foreseeable future.

Considering cultural collections and archives, similar trends may be evaluated and conclusions drawn as to the projected growth of future collections. As discussed in Issue C on archives, there are known collections to add to the museum collection in the near future. Issue A has discussed the ability of the parks to properly store and curate current and future collections over the next five to ten years. It is reasonable to assume that artifacts, specimens, objects, and archives will continue to be acquired for decades to come and that their addition to the museum collection will be a valuable asset to park resources.

Growth of the Museum Program

The museum program has taken many forms since the days when the parks were staffed by soldiers from the U.S. Army, rangers on horseback in the 1920s, and interpreters acting as collateral-duty curators in the 1970s. By the early 1990s, the parks had a journeyman-level museum curator and a museum technician to run the museum program. Since the last curator left in the mid-1990s, a single museum technician has managed the collections.

Numerous plans and reports helped guide the museum program over the last twenty-five years, and most of these have already been discussed in other issues in this plan (see Selected Bibliography). To a substantial extent, the recommendations made by these plans have not been implemented. This reflects the lack of funding, staff, and needed technical and professional skills required to perform the complex and substantial workload prescribed by these prior plans. The work that has been accomplished is impressive, and it is clear that the parks have a desire to manage their museum collections to professional standards.

Discussion

The growth of the museum and archival collections at SEKI has, for the most part, been supported by facilities and staffing that have sought to meet the challenge of organizing, documenting, preserving, and providing access to the collections. In recent years, the limitations of existing space and staffing have begun to create an urgent need to reorganize and increase efficiency, as discussed throughout this plan. This issue attempts to set forth a strategy for achieving the necessary improvements in a timely manner.

Growth of the Museum Collections

The growth of SEKI museum collections provides both a threat and an opportunity to the parks. The threat is that collections require additional storage space and labor-intensive processing, and can be disruptive to staff and overwhelm existing spaces. The opportunity is that growth increases the quantity and quality of the museum's holdings, which improves the possibilities for research, publications, exhibits, and interpretation, and it brings increased public and management appreciation of the value of the collection. The growth of the collection also helps justify additional project funding for cataloging, storage reorganization, staff training, and additional staff. The challenge is to manage the program in such a way that the workload is organized to bring increasing success and order in a timely manner, with measurable accomplishments and adequate support.

A large amount of material, primarily archives, has been identified as suitable for inclusion in the collection and should be accessioned. These materials are primarily park records and images. Archeology, ecology, and other park programs are also generating new collections. These new collections will require the reorganization of museum space to allow for more efficient processing, improved storage and access, and increased capacity for absorbing these newly accessioned materials.

Scope of Collection Statement

The draft Scope of Collection Statement (SOCS) should be revised to reflect updated approaches and new understandings of the need for collection acquisitions to fill gaps in subject coverage, expand usability, and improve overall quality (see Appendix D). A revised SOCS can incorporate language that discusses the nature of desired additions to the collection.

For historic materials, additions might have such qualities as:

- Known provenience or history.
- Significance and relevance to the park mission.
- Non-mass-produced, meaning they are handmade or modified.
- Rare or hard-to-find, such as early park history items, unpublished information, or materials associated with imminent persons.

Certainly historic documents and photographs directly related to the parks and over perhaps fifty years old should be highly desirable additions.

The archeology component of the SOCS should be updated by the park archeologist to reflect the legal and scholarly mandates and the goals of the parks' archeological program.

The biological and geological collections discussed in the SOCS need to incorporate a better discussion of voucher collections, Inventory and Monitoring, and especially outside permits and repositories. The SOCS needs to adopt a scientific approach to building high-quality scientific collections that document the flora and fauna of the parks' biota, with emphasis on systematic collections resulting from research and monitoring projects.

The program should consider using the SOCS as a working document, making notations whenever new evaluations contribute further refinements, and incorporating new approaches and topics as they arise. Then, every five to ten years, when a new emphasis is justified, the document can be completely revised using all the notations collected during the period of its active use.

Growth of the Museum Program

Museum programs grow in response to increasing need based on the size and complexity of the museum and archive collections, their preservation and use, and the benefits to other park programs and the public. A professionally-managed operation will encourage and support new acquisitions through better identifying needs and evaluations of potential accessions.

The parks should be able to meet urgent short-term goals by utilizing resources from a variety of sources, including park or regional funding and staff support, details of NPS curators, curator-of-record assistance, and in-house resources. There is justification and need to increase the knowledge, skills, and abilities of the current museum technician. Working on details with other NPS collections and experts is very cost-effective, and can complement formal training classes and attendance at conferences.

The parks need to consider upgrading the museum technician to a GS-9/11 Museum Curator when justified by accumulated duties and responsibilities. If the technician position becomes vacant, consider upgrading to a journeymen-level GS-11 Museum Curator. Sequoia and Kings Canyon collections justify a full-time permanent professional curator who has the knowledge and experience to independently manage the collections.

An archivist to do archival processing is needed. Initially, over the five-year period of this plan, this need may be met by a project-based or term archivist. In the future, there should be adequate justification for a permanent professional archivist GS-11 position.

New positions and upgrades are not easily created during periods of tight budgets. They take time and dedicated effort to pursue all avenues available. These needs will be supported as significant progress is made on the tasks outlined in this plan, and the parks' museum program is put on a sound management track toward being an effective professional steward of the marvelous treasures contained in the museum collection.

Recommendations

- Incorporate estimates of collections growth into all future project statements and plans for facilities, processing, and staffing. Evaluate the past growth of the collections and make assessments for their future growth.

- Revise the draft Scope of Collection Statement to include updated concepts and directions, and seek wider review from discipline specialists. Use the SOCS as a working document when evaluating all new accessions; record refinements and observations.

- Consider a fast-track approach to upgrading the museum program. Reorganize storage, offices, and processing spaces. Seek out training details for the museum technician. Bring in NPS curators and archivists on detail to address the backlog. The importance of collections to the parks should be supported by the Regional Strategy for Museum Facilities.

- Upgrade the current museum technician to a museum curator position. Long-term growth of the collections and museum program will only be feasible with a professional staff.

- Create archivist and support technician positions as soon as possible using project funds until such time as a base increase for the museum program is added to the park. Look for project-supported term positions where base-funded permanent positions are not feasible.

Sequoia and Kings Canyon National Parks Museum Management Plan

SECTION I

These questions will help determine use patterns for museum, archives, and library collections. For the purpose of this survey, a "visit" to the collections also includes verbal, telephone, and e-mail requests for information that would require the collections manager to find and communicate that information in return.

1. Do you use the park library? No (**4**) Yes (**26**)
   If Yes, about how many times in the last year? **223** total (**10** average)
2. Do you use the park collections/archives? No (**6**) Yes (**24**)
   If Yes, about how many times in the last year? **267** total (**12** average)
3. Do you use non-NPS libraries, collections or archives? No (**14**) Yes (16)
   If Yes, about how many times in the last year? **232** total (**17** average)
4. What parts of the park collections/archives do you use (check as many as apply):

Cultural Resource Collections

- Historic Archives and Records (Non-NPS) (**46%**)
- Park Cultural Resource Records (**33%**)
- Park Administrative Records (**63%**)
- Photographs and Images (**67%**)
- Archeological Artifacts and Materials (**25%**)
- Historic Artifacts and Objects (**21%**)
- Ethnological & Native American Collection (**13%**)

Natural Resource Collections

- Mammals and Birds (**4%**)
- Reptiles, Amphibians, Fishes
- Insects and Invertebrates (**8%**)
- Herbarium/Plants (**33%**)
- Paleontological Fossils and Traces (**8%**)
- Geological Rocks, Minerals, Samples (**8%**)
- Natural Records, Maps, Images, Reports (**63%**)

5. What are the primary reasons you use the collections (check as many as apply):

- Address Internal NPS information needs (**75%**)
- Address Non-NPS information needs (**33%**)
- Explore needs for new information (gaps) (**21%**)
- Develop Interpretive Programs (**33%**)
- Develop Exhibits (**25%**)

- Resource Management Research (**50%**)
- Maintenance/Repair Information (**8%**)
- Historic Structure Information (**21%**)
- Planning/Compliance Information (**29%**)
- Identification & Comparison (**33%**)

☐ Develop Publications	(21%)	☐	Personal Learning	(54%)
☐ Develop Inventory & Monitoring Programs	(13%)	☐	Other (list): Prescribed burn & wildfire data; Law enforcement documents	(8%)

SECTION II

We realize there might be many different reasons park staff may or may not make use of the museum, archives, or library collections in their work. Below are areas that may have problems and need improvements. Let us know where you think improvements are needed.

6.   What improvements are most needed? (check as many as apply):

☐	A. Expand the collections to contain artifacts, specimens, or information that I need	(17%)
☐	B. Combine collections with supporting archives and/or library references	(10%)
☐	C. Relocate the collections to a location more accessible to my location	(3%)
☐	D. Reorganize collections to make them more accessible	(20%)
☐	E. Improve electronic access to museum collection data and object information	(60%)
☐	F. Provide listings and finding aids of what is in the museum collection	(60%)
☐	G. Provide on-line or remote access to databases	(53%)
☐	H. Provide remote computer access to collections/archives	(23%)
☐	I. Provide a work area	
	☐ Wet lab	(53%)
	☐ Table space	(50%)
	☐ Other (Map layout)	(3%)
☐	J. Provide data access and a computer workstation.	(20%)

Other needs include:
    ☐ Printer   (13%)
    ☐ Copy machine   (13%)
    ☐ Scanner   (10%)
    ☐ Other:

☐	K. Staff collection with at least one professional position	(13%)
☐	L. Provide additional professional staff to assist collection users	(7%)
☐	M. Provide additional professional staff to organize and work on collections	(23%)
☐	N. Improve customer service provided by museum staff	(3%)
☐	O. Increase hours the museum collections are open	
☐	P. Improve the preservation and physical condition of the collections	(7%)
☐	Q. Other (please list):	(23%)

Training and knowledge of what is available. Improve Library Access. Make Access easier for staff. With alarm system collection is not available. Communicate services available to new employees & public access requirements. Provide keys. Help me find out how to use it.

7. In the list above, what are the highest priorities at the current time? (Use letters above)

    23% = I   20% = F   13% = E   10% = G, Q   7% = D

8. What are the second most important priorities for improvement?

    20% = E   13% = F, G, M   10% = I   7% = A, H

SECTION III

In order to assure a well-represented response from a cross section of park staff, we would appreciate a minimum amount of demographic information.

9. Number of years in the NPS   total = **473 years** Average = **16.3 years**
10. Number of years at current park   total = **306 years**
    Average = **10.2 years**
11. Number of years in current position   total = **195 years** Average = **6.5 years**
12. Current work assignment:
    Resource Management = **12**
    Interpretation = **6**
    Other = **5** (SNHA, Fire Management, Interdivisional, SNHA, Superintendent)
    Ranger = **4**
    Administration = **2**
    Maintenance = **1**
13. Are you currently:
    Permanent staff = **23**
    Term/Temporary = **4**
    Cooperating association = **3**
    Volunteer = **0**
    Seasonal = **0**
    Other = **0**
14. Please estimate the time you spent responding to this survey:
    Total = **215** minutes, average = **7.4** minutes

_____ NATIONAL PARK
MUSEUM COLLECTION ACCESS PROCEDURES

PURPOSE

It is the policy of the National Park Service, and of _____, that its natural and cultural resources be preserved for future generations and made available for educational and scholarly purposes. The principal value of the park's museum collection is as a resource of the park. The collection also possesses considerable research value and its use for research is always encouraged. In order to both preserve the collection and allow for use, the staff is charged with regulating access to the collections. This document serves as a guide to the staff in carrying out its responsibilities for both encouraging and regulating access to the collections and for meeting the needs of prospective researchers. This document should be reviewed every two years and revised as necessary for it to remain current and viable. Review it concurrently with review of the park's approved Scope of Collection Statement.

GENERAL ACCESS PROCEDURES

1. Except as otherwise noted below, this written procedural statement applies equally to museum objects, archival materials, and museum collection records. These procedures also apply to information about such park resources written by the staff in the course of their official duties.

2. Access to objects in the collection, to storage cabinets and exhibit cases, and to keys to locks on storage rooms, storage cabinets, and exhibit cases, will be strictly controlled by the superintendent. All areas thus controlled shall be identified as "Secure Areas."

3. Only those persons identified under "Eligibility for Access to Museum Collections" will be permitted access to secure areas under ordinary conditions. Under emergency conditions, emergency response personnel may have access to secure areas, but only under such conditions and with such supervision and control as the superintendent may establish in the park's Emergency Operations Plan.

4. The granting of access to a secure area does not automatically grant access to objects, archival materials, or records kept in those areas. Only persons with legitimate needs to use, study, photograph, or handle collection items will be granted access to them; other persons may be granted access only to rooms housing such items. A request for access must indicate whether the request applies only to a secure area or to both the area and the collections therein.

5. Because the physical integrity and safety of the collections are a primary park responsibility, no one will be granted unlimited, totally discretionary access to the collections except for the superintendent, chief of interpretation and resource management, museum curator, and the museum technician. These individuals are referred to as "authorized staff" in this policy

statement. Persons not so designated must be accompanied by authorized staff in order to gain legitimate access to the collections. Anyone's access can be denied or restricted by the superintendent at any time and for any reason. Any unforeseen questions or problems regarding access will be considered by the superintendent on a case-by-case basis.

6. All persons, except authorized staff, who request access to collections for the purposes of using or viewing objects, archival materials, or collections records must specify in their request which items or groups of items they will want to use. If permission to access the collections is granted, only those items will be made available. Persons already working with collections may verbally request access to additional items; their requests will be considered on a case-by-case basis.

ELIGIBILITY FOR ACCESS TO MUSEUM COLLECTIONS

Access to the collections should be granted by the superintendent to the following persons or classes of persons:

1. **Researchers**. All outside individuals requesting access to the collection for research purposes must submit a written request to the superintendent in advance of the visit. The request should include a short research proposal, the objects needed to be studied, the preferred date and time of the visit, and the researcher's full name, address, and telephone number. Prospective researchers should also:

    *   Submit documentation that he/she is affiliated with a recognized educational institution, either as faculty or as a registered student, or that he/she is on the staff of a recognized museum.
    *   Demonstrate in writing the need to study objects or records in the park's collections in order to conduct research.
    *   Demonstrate that the research to be conducted has merit, that it is not frivolous, and that the results of the research will benefit either the researcher's institution and/or the park.
    *   Make their research results available to the park in some form.

    All persons granted access under this item of eligibility must be accompanied at all times by authorized park staff.

2. **National Park Service staff from the Regional Office, the Washington Office, either of the design centers, or other parks who are visiting the park on official business.** The nature of their work must require them to evaluate, inspect, or work with the collections or the rooms, cabinets, or cases housing the collections or with park records on the collections. All persons granted access under this item of eligibility must be accompanied at all times by authorized park staff.

3. **Members of Native American groups having official business with the park staff for examining, handling, or appraising archeological or ethnographic objects in the collections.** The superintendent should ascertain that the individuals are tribal members, and not individuals who may or may not otherwise be eligible to request access on their own right (see below). Normally, when persons from a certain tribe are allowed access to the collections to use objects representing that tribe, they will not be allowed access to objects representing other tribes. Exceptions may be made on a case-by-case basis as necessary. All

persons granted access under this item of eligibility must be accompanied at all times by authorized park staff.

4. **Non-curatorial park employees, including volunteers, who are being oriented to the park and their work or who require access to collections as part of their internal training.** Such persons must be accompanied at all times by authorized park staff.

5. **Park maintenance and protection staff in the performance of their official duties.** Except in the most unusual circumstances, such personnel shall have access only to rooms in which collections are kept, and not to storage cabinets, exhibit cases, or key boxes. As provided below, other means shall be made available to these personnel for emergency access. Persons granted access under this item of eligibility must be accompanied at all times by authorized park staff.

Access to the collections by the following persons or classes of persons is discretionary but may be granted by the superintendent:

6. **Private individuals seeking to use the collection for research or study.** As noted above, all outside individuals requesting access to the collection for research purposes must submit a written request to the superintendent in advance of the visit. The request should include a short research proposal, the objects needed to be studied, the preferred date and time of the visit, and the researcher's full name, address, and telephone number. Private individuals seeking to use the collection for research or study must present credentials satisfactory to the superintendent that they have serious intent and are engaged in research which necessitates examination of objects or records at close hand. Persons granted access under this item of eligibility must be accompanied at all times by park staff.

7. **Individuals or representatives of organizations, institutions, or corporations desiring to use objects or records in the collection for commercial or publicity purposes.** Such persons must satisfy the superintendent that their purposes are legitimate and that the proposed uses are in keeping with park purposes and the NPS mission and will not reflect adversely on the park, the National Park Service, or a Native American tribe, if the request is for tribal materials. In addition, such persons must satisfy the superintendent that their purposes cannot be met by access to collections or institutions outside the park. Access should not be granted solely on the grounds that access to the park's collection would be more economical or "easier" for them than access to another collection. Persons granted access under this item of eligibility must be accompanied at all times by authorized staff.

8. **Employees of construction or service companies who require access to collection storage or exhibit areas in order to service or maintain the building or its utilities, including alarm systems.** Such persons will be allowed access only under the terms of a contract or purchase order issued by or for the park and only to those areas where they are supposed to work. Under no circumstances shall such persons be allowed unsupervised access to objects kept in storage cabinets and exhibit cases. All persons granted access under this item of eligibility must be accompanied at all times by authorized staff.

9. **Other persons or groups of persons may be allowed limited access to the collections on determination by the superintendent that such access will be to the mutual benefit of the persons or groups and the park.** Examples of circumstances to which this item of eligibility might apply include: tours for school classes; tours for members of museum organizations or historical societies; tours for families of park employees; orientation for

local political/governmental officials; orientation for visiting Park Service employees not on official business; tours for non-NPS museum personnel, teachers, and prospective researchers who are considering applying for permission to use or view the collection. All persons granted access under this item of eligibility must be accompanied at all times by park curatorial staff.

In applying the above items of eligibility, persons under 16 years of age generally should not be admitted to collection storage areas. That provision may be waived by the superintendent in respect to family members of park employees or when circumstances dictate that it may be waived without endangering collections. Authorized staff may allow access to members of their immediate families under 16 years of age without further permission; the staff person must accompany his/her family member(s) and will be held responsible for their conduct.

All organized groups of school-age children must be under the direct control of at least one adult (teacher or parent), and group size will be limited to five children. This policy does not apply to groups in exhibit areas open to the general public during regular visiting hours. This policy does apply to such groups outside of regular visiting hours, even in otherwise publicly accessible exhibit areas.

CONDITIONS OF ACCESS

The following conditions apply equally to all non-staff persons granted access to a secure area, unless so indicated to the contrary.

1. Access to a secure area will be allowed only during the park's regular operating hours, unless other arrangements have been made in advance of the visit.

2. The staff is obliged to consider requests for access only when requests are made in advance of the day of the visit. Therefore, persons needing to have access are urged to make their requests known to the superintendent as far in advance as possible.

3. Prospective visitors should be aware that the park staff is extremely busy at certain times of the year and that authorized staff may not be available to assist them at those times. Accordingly, it is suggested that persons needing access offer or be prepared to discuss alternative times with the staff when they submit their requests.

4   The park's decision to allow access may depend upon the availability of space for the requester to work. The park attempts to keep at least some space available at all times for visiting researchers. However, if one researcher already has been accommodated, there might not be space for others at the same time. Space availability also might be affected by in-house activities, such as inventorying collections, cleaning exhibits, and staff research activities.

5. All guidelines for handling artifacts and archival materials must be followed by all collection users, whether staff or non-staff. Those guidelines are published separately and may be requested in advance of a visit. A copy of the guidelines also will be provided to each user at the time he/she arrives.

6. All persons, staff and non-staff alike, must sign in and out of the collection storage area on the "Collections Access Log." A sample page from the log is attached to these procedures (see Appendix B-2). The log book is located directly inside the door of the storage area.

7.   All non-staff visitors and all staff visitors who are not designated as "authorized staff" must be accompanied at all times by authorized staff when in museum collection storage areas or when working in open exhibits.

8.   The park reserves the right to require a third-party recommendation for any individual who desires access to the collections and is not already known to the staff.

9.   The park reserves the right to receive the following as a condition for granting access to the collections:

   a.   Copies of any notes, measured drawings, or photographs taken on or of objects or records in the collections.

   b.   Copies of completed research papers and publications derived from work on the collections.

   c.   Copies of completed research papers and publications when they contain photographs of objects in the collections or facsimile copies of documents in the archival collections.

   d.   Copies of any reports or publications based solely or largely on research conducted on the collections.

Copies of formal reports and other published materials shall be provided at the researcher's expense. Copies of notes, drawings, photographs, and other products of research shall be provided at the researcher's expense, except when doing so constitutes an economic burden, in which case the superintendent can elect to defray those costs or waive the requirement for the researcher to provide the materials.

Under no circumstances, excepting emergencies, will persons other than authorized staff possess, carry, use, or otherwise have access to keys to locks on storage rooms, storage cabinets, exhibit cases, and other places where museum objects, archival materials, or museum collection records are kept. This rule also applies to combinations of locks on safes and vaults.

USE OF THE COLLECTION

Except in the case of loans to qualified museums or educational institutions, no museum objects from the park's collection should be removed from storage or exhibit for the purposes of research or examination. All research utilizing collection items should be conducted in the collection storage area or exhibit location, and all researchers not designated as authorized staff must be accompanied at all times by authorized staff.

Should the need arise, the superintendent may allow for a limited number of archival materials or photographs to be transported to either the office of the superintendent, or that of the chief of Interpretation and Resource Management, for research and/or reproduction purposes. Any such materials removed from storage or exhibit shall be tracked by signed receipt (see Appendix B-1), and the item will be returned to the proper location by the end of the day that it was moved (place receipt in the location that the item was removed from).

Any museum objects that must be photographed or otherwise reproduced off-site (e.g., archival materials to be reproduced for publication or exhibit purposes at a photographer's studio) must be tracked by signed receipt and approved by the superintendent (see Appendix B-1). The photographer or other person working with said item must sign a DI-105, Receipt for Property form. These forms, when completed, are to be filed in the proper accession folder until the item is returned to the park.

Appendix B-1

_____ NATIONAL PARK
MUSEUM COLLECTION
TEMPORARY REMOVAL SLIP

Note: This form must be filled out before any objects from the park's museum collection are removed from storage or exhibit for the purposes of research or reproduction.

The following item:

_____

(print item name and catalog number)

has been temporarily removed to:_____

for the purpose of: (circle one)   reproduction   research

Removed by:

_____

(Print name & title, sign, and date)

Superintendent must approve of all museum objects temporarily removed to an off-site location:

Approved by:

_____

(Superintendent signature and date)

Appendix B-2

NATIONAL PARK
MUSEUM COLLECTION ACCESS LOG

NAME	ORGANIZATION/ADDRESS	DATE	TIME IN/OUT	REASON FOR ENTRY

**NEPA COMPLIANCE PROJECT CHECKLIST
FOR ETHNOGRAPHIC / ORAL HISTORY PROJECTS
(per *DO#28, Cultural Resources Management Guideline*, Chapter 10, p. 165)**

Project Title: _____

Project Number: _____   PMIS Number: _____

Contractor/Implementation Supervisor: _____

Company/Agency: _____

Project Start and Completion Dates: _____

Return copy of completed checklist upon completion/close-out of project. Submit completed project file, with the checklist sheet attached to the project file.

- ☐   Field notes (summaries of)
- ☐   Informed Consent Release Forms
- ☐   Oral history audio tapes
- ☐   Transcripts
- ☐   Videotapes
- ☐   Photographs
- ☐   Copies of contracts, change orders
- ☐   Copies of cooperative agreement
- ☐   Correspondence (including e-mail)
- ☐   Draft report
- ☐   Final report
- ☐   Publications

Date Received in RPPS/Compliance: _____

Initials: _____

NEPA COMPLIANCE PROJECT CHECKLIST
FOR MAINTENANCE and CONSTRUCTION

Project Title: _____

Project Number: _____   PMIS Number: _____

Contractor/Implementation Supervisor: _____

Company/Agency: _____

Project Start and Completion Dates: _____

PROJECT MANAGEMENT

CURRENT WORK
- ☐ Correspondence
- ☐ Meeting Notes
- ☐ Schedules
- ☐ Budgets & Cost Estimates
- ☐ Task Orders & Consultant Contracts
- ☐ Compliance & Approvals
- ☐ Documentation & Photographs
- ☐ Other

EXISTING INFORMATION
- ☐ Planning Documents
- ☐ Historical Research Comments
- ☐ Infrastructure Info/Evaluations
- ☐ Site Info/Evaluations Comments
- ☐ Building Info/Evaluations
- ☐ Market Research & Financial Analysis
- ☐ Agreements & Lease Documents
- ☐ Other

RESEARCH & WRITING
- ☐ Research Materials
- ☐ Graphics
- ☐ Preliminary Drafts & Comments
- ☐ Final Draft & Comments
- ☐ Other

PLANNING

C.O.R. FILES
- ☐ Established by COR on project-by-project basis

- ☐ Scoping
- ☐ Data Collection
- ☐ Public Review & Comments
- ☐ Draft Plan
- ☐ Final Plan/Staff Report/FONSI
- ☐ Alternatives Form/Design Review
- ☐ Other

DESIGN
- ☐ Schematic Design & Review Comments
- ☐ Design Development & Review

- ☐ Construction Docs & Review

- ☐ Materials Research (break out if needed)
- ☐ Outline Specifications
- ☐ Specifications (break out by CSI format)
- ☐ Other

BIDDING & CONSTRUCTION
- ☐ Bids & Revised Cost Estimates
- ☐ Submittals (break out by CSI format)
- ☐ Inspection Records, Photos & Reports
- ☐ Change Orders
- ☐ Operating Manuals, Warranties
- ☐ Construction Close-out
- ☐ Post Occupancy Inspections
- ☐ Other

Date Received in RPPS/Compliance: _____

Initials: _____

**NEPA COMPLIANCE PROJECT CHECKLIST
FOR INTERPRETATION EXHIBITS AND PLANS**

Project Title: _____

Project Number: _____   PMIS Number: _____

Contractor/Implementation Supervisor: _____

Company/Agency: _____

Project Start and Completion Dates: _____

Return copy of completed checklist upon completion/close-out of project.

PROJECT MANAGEMENT
- ☐ Correspondence (including email)
- ☐ Meeting Notes
- ☐ Schedules

- ☐ Task Orders & Consultant Contracts
- ☐ Documentation & Photographs
- ☐ Other

EXISTING INFORMATION
- ☐ Planning Documents
- ☐ Historical Research
- ☐ Infrastructure Info/Evaluations
- ☐ Site Info/Evaluations
- ☐ Building Info/Evaluations
- ☐ Other

RESEARCH & WRITING
- ☐ Research Materials
- ☐ Graphics
- ☐ Preliminary Drafts & Comments
- ☐ Final Draft & Comments
- ☐ Other

DESIGN
- ☐ Schematic Design & Review Comments
- ☐ Design Development & Review Comments
- ☐ Budgets & Cost Estimates
- ☐ Construction Docs & Review Comments

- ☐ Materials Research (break out if needed)
- ☐ Outline Specifications
- ☐ Specifications (break out by CSI format)
- ☐ Alternatives Form/Design Review
- ☐ Other

BIDDING & CONSTRUCTION
- ☐ Bids & Revised Cost Estimates
- ☐ Submittals
- ☐ Inspection Records, Photos & Reports
- ☐ Change Orders
- ☐ Construction Close-out
- ☐ Other

OBJECT CONSERVATION
- ☐ Correspondence (including email)
- ☐ Treatment Reports
- ☐ Photographs

Date Received in RPPS/Compliance: _____

Initials: _____

NEPA COMPLIANCE PROJECT CHECKLIST
FOR
BASIC SECTION 106 COMPLIANCE
(per *DO#28, Cultural Resources Management Guideline*, Chapter 5, p. 60 and Appendix P, p. 307)

Project Title: _____

Project Number: _____   PMIS Number: _____

Contractor/Implementation Supervisor: _____

Company/Agency: _____

Project Start and Completion Dates: _____

Return copy of completed checklist and all paper and electronic documentation regarding decision upon compilation/close-out of project.

☐   Documentation of no-effect findings
☐   All evidence of consultation with the State Historic Preservation Officers (SHPOs) must be retained. Include hard copies of all electronic correspondence.
☐   "Assessment of Effect" forms
☐   Other 106 documentation
☐   Correspondence
☐   Plans
☐   Photographic images

Date Received in RPPS/Compliance: _____

Initials: _____

NEPA COMPLIANCE PROJECT CHECKLIST
FOR ARCHEOLOGY
(per *DO#28, Cultural Resources Management Guideline*, Chapter 6, p. 86)

Project Title: _____

Project Number: _____   PMIS Number: _____

Contractor/Implementation Supervisor: _____

Company/Agency: _____

Project Start and Completion Dates: _____

Return copy of completed checklist upon completion/close-out of project. Submit completed project file, with checklist sheet attached to project file. Artifacts and project documents to be curated at the Southeast Archeological Center (SEAC).

- ☐ Artifacts
- ☐ Copy of ARPA Permit (from SEAC)
- ☐ Field notes (Copies)
- ☐ Catalog records (to NPS standards – if over 1 cu. ft. of artifacts recovered, otherwise cataloged at SEAC)
- ☐ Final report
- ☐ Maps
- ☐ Drawings
- ☐ Photographs, negatives, slides (Film based required for project documentation)
- ☐ Digital photographic images (For reference use copies only)
- ☐ Videotapes
- ☐ Remote sensing data
- ☐ Copies of contracts, change orders
- ☐ Copies of cooperative agreement
- ☐ Correspondence (including e-mail)
- ☐ Repository agreements
- ☐ Specialists' reports and analyses
- ☐ Reports and manuscripts
- ☐ Artifact inventories
- ☐ Field specimen logs
- ☐ Analytical study data
- ☐ Computer documentation and data
- ☐ Conservation treatment records
- ☐ Reports on all scientific samples lost through destructive analysis

Date Received in RPPS/Compliance: _____

Initials: _____

NEPA COMPLIANCE PROJECT CHECKLIST
FOR LANDSCAPES / CULTURAL LANDSCAPES
(per *DO#28, Cultural Resources Management Guideline*, Chapter 7, p. 111)

Project Title: _____

Project Number: _____   PMIS Number: _____

Contractor/Implementation Supervisor: _____

Company/Agency: _____

Project Start and Completion Dates: _____

Return copy of completed checklist upon completion/close-out of project.

- □   All associated records
- □   Maps
- □   Plans
- □   Sketches
- □   Field notes
- □   Photographs, negatives, slides (Film based required for project documentation)
- □   Digital photographic images (For reference use copies only)
- □   Videotapes
- □   Soil or pollen analyses
- □   Construction files
- □   Copies of contracts, change orders
- □   Copies of cooperative agreement
- □   Correspondence (including e-mail)
- □   Cultural Landscape Report
- □   Other reports
- □   Publications
- □   Record of treatment (copy; including all specifications, plans, work procedures)

Date Received in RPPS/Compliance: _____

Initials: _____

NEPA COMPLIANCE PROJECT CHECKLIST
FOR
HISTORIC STRUCTURES
(per *DO#28, Cultural Resources Management Guideline*, Chapter 8, p. 136)

Project Title: _____

Project Number: _____ PMIS Number: _____

Contractor/Implementation Supervisor: _____

Company/Agency: _____

Project Start and Completion Dates: _____

Return copy of completed checklist upon completion/close-out of project. Submit completed project file with the checklist sheet attached to the project file. Material samples to be cataloged into park museum collection.

☐ Material (structure) samples
☐ Field notes
☐ Photographs, negatives, slides (Film based required for project documentation
☐ Digital photographic images (For reference use copies only)
☐ Videotapes
☐ Copies of contracts, change orders
☐ Copies of cooperative agreement
☐ Correspondence (including e-mail)
☐ Construction Files (including all plans and specifications)
☐ Reports
☐ Publications

Date Received in RPPS/Compliance: _____

Initials: _____

NEPA COMPLIANCE PROJECT CHECKLIST
FOR NATURAL RESOURCES
(per *NPS-77, Natural Resources Management Guideline*, Chapter 5, p. 53)

Project Title: _____

Project Number: _____   PMIS Number: _____

Contractor/Implementation Supervisor: _____

Company/Agency: _____

Project Start and Completion Dates: _____

Return copy of completed checklist upon completion/close-out of project. Submit completed project file, with the checklist sheet attached to the project file. All specimens to be cataloged into museum collection, but may be deposited in non-NPS repository.

- ☐ Field notes (NPS staff – originals; contractors – copies)
- ☐ NPS Collection Permit
- ☐ Catalog records
- ☐ Daily journals
- ☐ Maps
- ☐ Drawings
- ☐ Photographs, negatives, slides (Film based required for project documentation)
- ☐ Digital photographic images (For reference use copies only)
- ☐ Videotapes
- ☐ Raw data sheets
- ☐ Remote sensing data
- ☐ Copies of contracts, change orders
- ☐ Copies of cooperative agreement
- ☐ Correspondence
- ☐ Repository agreements
- ☐ Specialists' reports and analyses
- ☐ Reports and manuscripts
- ☐ Collection inventories
- ☐ Field catalogs
- ☐ Analytical study data
- ☐ Sound recordings
- ☐ Computer documentation and data
- ☐ Tabulations and lists
- ☐ Specimen preparation records
- ☐ Conservation treatment records
- ☐ Reports on all scientific samples lost through destructive analysis

Date Received in RPPS/Compliance: _____

Initials: _____

NEPA COMPLIANCE DOCUMENT CHECKLIST
FOR RP & PS PROJECT FILE
(per *DO#12, Conservation Planning and Environmental Impact Analysis Handbook*, Chapter 2-12, Administrative Record)

Project Title: _____

Project Number: _____ PMIS Number: _____

Contractor/Implementation Supervisor: _____

Company/Agency: _____

Project Start and Completion Dates: _____

- ☐ Meeting notes regarding content, issues, alternatives, etc., of EA/EIS
- ☐ Minutes of meetings of public involvement
- ☐ Letters of public involvement
- ☐ Telephone call notes of public involvement
- ☐ EA for review
- ☐ Environmental Impact Statement (EIS) for review
- ☐ Approval letter to implementing division
- ☐ Copy of contract
- ☐ Copy of cooperative agreement
- ☐ Specifications
- ☐ Plans, maps
- ☐ Close-outs
- ☐ Copy of ARPA Permit
- ☐ Copy of finding of no effect from SHPO

Date Received in RPPS/Compliance: _____

Initials: _____

Mandated Retained Records for Denver Service Center (DSC) Projects

Park:_____ Package Number:_____
Project Type Information: _____
Sensitive Data Present (indicate report): _____
Contract Number: _____

Project Information Files
☐ Correspondence that documents decisions
☐ Project agreements
☐ Discussions about design changes
☐ Meeting notes
☐ Specifications
☐ Cost estimates
☐ Compliance information
☐ Draft documents and drawings
☐ Review process information including transmittals

Any of these documents with original signatures are the record copies. DSC/NPS is required by law to keep the record copies organized and retrievable per FOIA law 5 USC 552 and 44 USC 3301.

Contract Files
☐ Submittals
☐ Samples of materials used in projects
☐ Contracts
☐ Specifications
☐ Contract amendments and modifications with original signatures
☐ Justifications for contract changes
☐ Contract payrolls
☐ Contract field files
☐ Construction dailies
☐ Task orders
☐ Construction correspondence
☐ Documentation for contract disputes

NPS Technical Reports   Drawings
☐ Hazardous material reports
☐ Findings of no significant impact
☐ O&M manuals
☐ Value analysis reports
☐ Post occupancy evaluations
☐ Public involvement documents
☐ Concessions management plans
☐ General management plans
☐ Historic structure evaluations
☐ New area studies
☐ Resource management reports
☐ Special studies
☐ Environmental assessments, etc.

☐ Review copies
☐ Bid sets
☐ Amendments
☐ Negotiated modifications
☐ As-constructed drawings ("as-builts")

Information in the project files that is protected by FOIA from release to the public, e.g., the names of sub-contractors, cost estimates prior to the contract award, cost figures after the contract is awarded, social security numbers, some compliance information including some hazmat information, location of sensitive archaeological sites, etc.

The following is an excerpt of a section of the recent draft Scope of Collection Statement that deals with the descriptions and collecting goals for the different museum disciplines. See discussion of these topics in Issue D - Growth.

SOCS 2005 Draft

II. TYPES OF COLLECTIONS

A. Natural History Collection

The collection and maintenance of natural history specimens and all associated records in the parks' museum collection support the parks' research and resource management program. The natural history collection may include reference collections of species indigenous to the parks, synoptic collections for distribution, baseline monitoring, voucher specimens, and environmental monitoring samples.

1. Biology

Biological collections will be made only as needed, through bona fide research projects or passive collecting techniques (e.g., road kill or found dead), in accordance with 36 CFR 2.5 and the NPS Organic Act. The collection of rare, threatened, and endangered plant and animal species will comply with NPS Management Policies and also be in accordance with provisions of the Endangered Species Act of 1973 (amended). Such collection will be strictly limited according to the applicable rules of the U.S. Fish and Wildlife Service (USFWS) and the NPS. As of 1998, the park museum contains approximately 11,000 biological specimens; the majority and the most heavily used are those contained in the herbarium.

a. Microscopic Organisms

Included in this category are Monera and Protista organisms, of which no specimens are represented in the museum collection. Future collection will depend on research needs.

b. Plants

As used in this Scope, the term plant shall refer to all Plantae organisms including molds, fungi, lichens, mosses, liverworts, ferns, fern allies, conifers, and anthophyta. The parks' herbarium shall contain a complete representation of all native plants, as well as established exotic plants, found within these parks. Native plants should be represented by both flowering and fruiting phases and identification should be to the most specific level (e.g., sub-species). When practicable, and as more space becomes available, the collection and maintenance of multiple specimens will be encouraged; this will allow for the study of range and variation.

Twenty-four of the approximately 1,200 species of plants present in the parks are listed as sensitive. These are species identified as candidates for threatened or endangered status on the USFWS list or plants that are unique or rare in the parks. A complete and current listing will be kept with this Scope of Collection for reference. A voucher specimen for each population of federally listed, threatened plant will be acquired only from qualified field workers and must be fully documented.

At this time, floral specimens are cataloged by the collecting agency, whether NPS staff or Biological Resources Division of the USGS, and then turned over to the museum for curation. The maintenance and preservation of this collection is one of the most important functions of the park museum collection. As more space eventually becomes available, the percentage given over to the curation of plant specimens should increase proportionally.

c. Invertebrates

As used in this Scope, the term invertebrates shall refer to aquatic and terrestrial organisms including sponges, worms, molluscs, anthropods, crustaceans, insects, etc. Other than the twelve cases of Lepidoptera and ten cases of cave-dwelling anthropods, the invertebrate community of the parks is represented by a relatively small number of specimens. The expansion of this collection is not identified as a priority and will remain dependent upon future research needs and the activities of the Division of Natural Resources.

d. Vertebrates

The primary collection of vertebrates for the region is housed in the Museum of Vertebrate Zoology at the University of California, Berkeley. A directory of their collections from Fresno and Tulare Counties will be obtained and kept in the collection record. Ninety species of mammals, 195 species of birds, 25 species of reptiles, fifteen species of amphibians, and nine species of fish are known to exist in the parks. Less than 25% of these are represented in the parks' museum.

e. Field Records, Data and Reports

All records associated with specimens collected in conjunction with biological research must be maintained with the specimens as part of the museum collection.

f. Research Specimens (36 CFR 2.5)

Specimens and associated field data and records generated as a result of approved research projects conducted by non-NPS staff are included in this category. The repository and responsibility for curation of any collections resulting from a research project will be determined prior to the issuance of a permit and recorded in the accession file.

2. Geology

As of 1998, the collection contains some 400 geologic specimens. At present, the acquisition of geologic specimens is not identified as a priority. Until such time as the expansion of this collection is deemed necessary by a professional authority, collection will only take place under passive condition or under the auspices of specific research projects.

a. Rocks and Minerals

If deemed significant enough to warrant collection, the collection may contain no more than two characteristic, hand-sized samples of each formation and mappable unit. Included are igneous, sedimentary, metamorphic, and fault-zone material.

Cave formations will be treated as endangered or irreplaceable rocks with samples collected only under passive conditions or as a result of specific research projects and in consultation with the parks' Cave Specialist.

b. Surface Process Samples

If deemed significant enough to warrant collection, the collection may contain samples of types of surface action and result. These may include glacial striation and polish, wind, stream, and lake action, deposits or abraded stones.

c. Field Records, Data and Reports

All records associated with specimens collected in conjunction with geological research must be maintained with the specimens as part of the museum collection.

3. Paleontology

The paleontology collection totals twenty in number and includes a small number of fossils from the Mineral King roof Pendant as well as samples of fossil sequoia trees from outside of the parks. Each paleontological specimen is unique and irreplaceable and is to be treated in a similar manner to archeological material. Any uncontrolled surface collection by staff and visitors is to be strongly discouraged. Future collection will be based on a professionally identified need to expand in this area. As with all museum collections, associated records will remain in the museum.

B. Cultural Resources Collection

The collection contains material from the disciplines of archeology, ethnology, and history and includes holographic and other documentary material, photographs, fine art, and historic objects.

Objects and documentary material related to the history of Sequoia and Kings Canyon National Parks are collected subject to limitations of space and NPS management policy concerning the retention of records. Objects with a direct tie to the parks are deemed more desirable than those with an indirect, or contextual association. Objects without documented connections to Sequoia and Kings Canyon National Parks will be secured only for specific exhibition or study needs and only when documented material is not available.

1. Archeology

Archeological collections are primarily generated in response to cultural resource management requirements and by research under the Archeological Resources Protection Act of 1979. The archeological collection includes artifacts and other material obtained using recognized archeological methods and under approved project research designs. As of 2004, the collection numbers some 18,000 items. It is anticipated that the collections will continue to grow in this direction, especially since the archeological surveying of the parks by NPS staff is ongoing.

a. Artifacts and Other Specimens

Park staff and visitors should be discouraged from picking up surface finds. Artifacts should not be removed by their finder, but should be reported to park staff. If materials are turned in to park staff, provenience information should be obtained from the finder and the artifact and the documentation should be routed to the parks' Cultural Resources Specialist. Artifacts will be recovered only by controlled archeological method: material with a clearly established and datable typology, such as projectile points, obsidian samples for typing and hydration, or material under immediate threat of loss or destruction, will be collected. Such material, when collected, will be cataloged into the collection. In all other cases, the preference will be to thoroughly document the find and to leave artifacts in place.

Prehistoric material. The parks have a small but valuable collection of prehistoric material. Consisting primarily of field-collected lithics, the collection also contains pottery, including several complete Owens Valley brownware vessels, and several steatite artifacts. While the expressed preference is to leave artifacts on site, active collection will take place when the threat to the artifact's endurance is understood to be imminent or when deemed necessary for the furtherance of the objectives of specific and approved research projects.

Historic material. The collection of historic archeological material is small. At present, it consists primarily of a recovered cache left by Orland Bartholomew, an adventurer who skied the Sierra crest from Sequoia to

Yosemite in 1929. Other artifacts preserve aspects of the material culture of the miners and loggers who represent the initial European presence in the region.

b. Associated Records

As with all other collections, supporting records are retained and maintained as part of the museum collection. These records may include field notes, maps and drawings, catalogs, daily journals, photographs and negatives, slides, raw data sheets, instrument charts, and remote sensing data, as well as any other documentation generated through archeological activity. These documents may contain sensitive information and their circulation is controlled.

2. Ethnology

At present, the parks' ethnographic collection centers upon the Agnew Collection, consisting of 28 Yokuts basket, a number of beads, and various utensils. This collection preserves valuable traces of Yokuts material culture. As discussed in the museum history, this collection originally included many more items and only those of local significance have been retained.

Future acquisitions of ethnographic material will be limited to artifacts that represent the peoples who formerly inhabited the area now maintained as Sequoia & Kings Canyon National Parks and those immediately adjacent. Appropriate groups would be the Wukchumni (or Inyana) Yokuts, the Monache (or Western Mono), and such Paiute groups as Big Pine, Bishop, and Fort Independence. As with all museum collections, associated records will remain in the museum.

3. History

The museum's historical collections are the largest of the museum's holdings. Including the archives, this collection contains nearly 300,000 items and is heavily used by researchers from inside and outside the parks. Further acquisitions will be made in accordance with the National Park Service Retention Schedule, the National Archives and Records Administration schedules and through gifts to the National Park Service.

The museum's historic photo-file has grown from the initial collection of works by the early photographic concessionaire, Lindley Eddy. Other commercial photographers now represented in the collections include General Grant concessionaire, Henry E. Roberts, as well as R.A. Underwood, the Laval Company, and Frasher's Photos. The logging history of the region is documented in early photographs by Roberts, N.E. Beckwith, and C.C. Curtis. A record of the natural history of the parks is preserved in photographs by the geologist Francois Matthes, the botanist Carl Sharsmith, and park naturalists Lowell Sumner and Howard Stagner. Other park employees, like John Diehl, have left an important photographic record of park engineering projects and trail construction.

Additionally, the collections contain: thirty-five years of prescribed-fire history; documents and artifacts from the era of military administration; uniforms, publications, and memorabilia from the Civilian Conservation Corps' tenure; and documents and artifacts from eighty years of Park Service development and administration.

a. Park History

As in the ethnological material, historical items will be accepted only if they relate directly to the people or events that are of significance to these parks. Important subjects include: the Kaweah Colony and associated events; the history of NPS management; Sierran vernacular architecture; the Civilian Conservation Corps; and the development of park concessions. Individual items may include: uniforms, either of the type, or those actually worn in the parks; documents; photographs; signs; tools; early literature; samples of building materials (paint, wood, fasteners, etc.); and curios and souvenirs of the parks.

b. Archives

Museum staff works with the parks' records manager in the maintenance and disposition of park records. Non-current records are retired to a secure loft space in the Ash Mountain warehouse for the duration of their scheduled retention. These records are periodically surveyed and those deemed to be of permanent value to the parks are brought into the archives. As defined by the *Museum Handbook*, such value may be understood as associational, evidential, administrative, artifactual, informational, or monetary; in all cases, value will be in relation to the parks' resources, administration, and history. Museum staff may find it useful to seek the advice of local subject matter specialists to assist in the determination of value. Further guidance may be found in the Sequoia and Kings Canyon Archival Assessment (1998) and the archives and manuscripts chapter of the Collections Management Plan (1994).

Accessions to the parks' archives will be made in accordance with *Director's Order #19*. Cataloging will follow the established avenues as expressed in the above-mentioned documents, the *Museum Handbook*, and the Sequoia and Kings Canyon National Parks Archives Guidelines (1996). The archives are organized into four artificial collections: manuscripts, catalog documents, oral history and park files. In the case of the last of these, an effort is to be made to duplicate the structure of the parks' administrative organization. A complete outline of how the archival collections are organized and processed is kept under separate binder.

c. Fine Art

Original art work, limited edition works, and commercial art work will be collected if it is the work of an individual or studio employed by or active in the parks, if the scene represented is of use as a research tool, or if the work is manifestly linked to the history or character of these parks.

d. Associated Records

All records associated with the history collection will be considered museum property and will be handled in an appropriate manner.

Selected Bibliography

Canadian Conservation Institute. *Framework for Preservation of Museum Collections, Agents of Deterioration.*

Eldredge, W. *In the Summer of 1903, Colonel Charles Young and the Buffalo Soldiers in Sequoia National Park.* Sequoia Natural History Association, 2003.

Sequoia & Kings Canyon National Parks. *Collection Management Plan.* Three Rivers, CA: National Park Service, 1997.

_____. *Collection Storage Plan,* draft. 1997.

_____. *Resource Management Plan.* 1999.

_____. *General Management Plan and Environmental Impact Statement.* 2006

_____. *Business Plan.* 2003.

_____. *Preventive Maintenance Plan.* 2004.

_____. *Scope of Collection Statement, draft.* 2005.

Strong, D.H. *From Pioneers to Preservationists: A Brief History of Sequoia and Kings Canyon National Parks.* Sequoia Natural History Association, 2000.

Voeks, Gretchen L. and Grace L. Katterman. *SEKI Collection Condition Survey.* Tucson: Western Archeological and Conservation Center, National Park Service, 1997.

Tweed, W. C. *Sequoia & Kings Canyon, The Story Behind the Scenery.* Las Vegas: KC Publishing, 2003.